BOOK ÆND
324 E. STATE
JACKSONVILLE, ILL. 62650

THE STATE FAIR BLUE RIBBON COOKBOOK

Prize Winning Recipes

by

Opal M. Hayes

An ETC Publication

CIP

Library of Congress Cataloging in Publication Data

Hayes, Opal M.   1897-
   The State fair blue ribbon cookbook.

   Includes index.
   1. Cookery.   2. Canning and preserving.   I. Title

TK715 .H3953

ISBN 0-88280-046-9

No part of this publication may be reproduced or transmitted in any form or by any means, electronic or mechanical, including photocopy, recording, or any information storage and retrieval system known or to be invented, without permission in writing from the publisher, except by a reviewer who wishes to quote brief passages in connection with a review written for inclusion in a magazine, periodical, newspaper, or broadcast.

Copyright © 1976 by ETC PUBLICATIONS
Palm Springs, California 92262

All rights reserved.

Printed in the United States of America

Table of Contents

Yeast Breads	1
Quick Breads	11
Cookies and Bars	19
Cakes	33
Icings	53
Pies and Cobblers	57
Honey Recipes	67
Desserts and Salads	77
Candies	83
Casseroles and Soup	87
Preserves, Jams, Jellies, and Butters	95
Pickles and Relishes	103
Home Canning	111
Household Hints and Homemade Soap	117
Index	121

*I hope everyone who uses my book
will enjoy trying my recipes
as much as I have enjoyed creating them.*

Opal M. Hayes

YEAST BREADS

YEAST BREADS

FROSTED CURRANT BREAD

2 cakes or 2 pkgs. dry yeast	2/3 cup sugar
2 T sugar	1 tsp. salt
2 cups scalded milk, cooled	2 eggs, well beaten
7 cups sifted flour	2/3 cup currants or raisins
1/2 cup margarine	

Dissolve yeast and 2 T sugar in cooled milk. Add 3 cups flour to make a sponge. Beat till smooth, cover and let rise one hour. Add softened margarine, sugar, and salt to sponge. Add eggs, currants and enough flour to make a soft dough and knead lightly. Place in a greased bowl and cover. Let rise until doubled. Knead down, shape into three loaves, let rise till light. Bake at 350º for 40 - 45 minutes. When almost cool, ice.

ICING:

2 T margarine, a little cream, and enough powdered sugar to thicken. Mix well and spread on cooled bread.

I hope you try this one. It is so good. It was a winner again in 1975, at the Illinois State Fair. The Judge wrote on my entry tag, "Excellent."

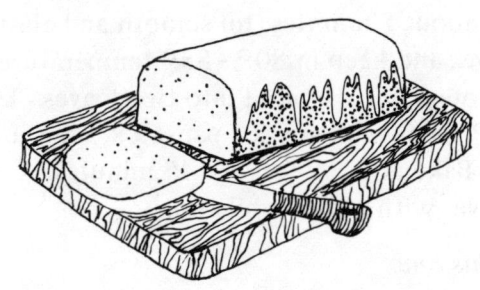

CINNAMON SWIRL ORANGE BREAD

1 pkg. dry yeast	1/2 cup milk
2 T warm water	1/4 cup sugar
2 T shortening	1 tsp. salt
1 tsp. grated orange rind	1/4 cup orange juice
1 medium egg, beaten	3 1/2 cups sifted flour
2 T sugar	1/2 tsp. cinnamon

Dissolve 1 pkg. of dry yeast in 2 T warm water. Scald 1/2 cup milk, add 1/4 cup sugar, 2 T shortening, 1 tsp. salt, 1 tsp. grated orange rind, 1/4 cup orange juice, 1 medium egg, beaten, and yeast. Add part of flour and beat well, then work in rest of flour on dough board. Knead about five minutes. Put in greased bowl, let rise in warm place about two hours. Roll out on floured board and spread with 2 T sugar, 1/2 tsp. cinnamon. Roll up as a jelly roll, seal edges, put in pan, 8 x 4 x 3, let rise. Bake at 325º for 45 minutes. Ice with powdered sugar icing.

•|•

CHEESE BREAD

1 pkg. dry yeast	1 tsp. salt
1/4 cup warm water	2 T shortening
1 3/4 cups scalded milk	1 1/2 cups grated cheese
3 T sugar	5 1/4 cups sifted flour

Soak yeast in 1/4 cup warm water. Add cheese and shortening to hot milk. Let cool. Add yeast mixture. Add 1 cup flour and beat till smooth. Add remaining flour, stir till smooth, put on floured board and knead about 5 minutes, till smooth and elastic. Put in greased bowl, cover and keep in 80º - 85º temperature, till double in bulk. Divide dough in half, mold into two loaves. Use the rolled dough method. Place in well greased pans, 9 x 5 x 3 inches. Let rise till doubled. Bake at 375º for 40 - 45 minutes. Cool on rack. Grease top of loaves with butter while hot.

I hope you try this one.

POTATO WHITE BREAD

Cook two potatoes, the size of eggs, in 1 cup of water. Run potatoes through sieve or strainer into potato water, cool.

- 1 cake of yeast
- 4 tsp. salt
- 11 cups sifted flour (about)
- 1/2 cup sugar
- 1/4 cup melted shortening

Measure potato and water. Add more warm water to make 4 cups. Add sugar to liquid. Dissolve yeast in liquid. Mix in part of flour. Beat till smooth. Add salt and shortening. Add last of flour, leave some to use on board. Knead on board with a little flour for about 10 minutes. Put in large greased bowl or pan. Let rise till double in bulk in a warm place. Punch down and turn dough over and divide dough into four loaves. Have four 1 lb. size pans greased. I like to roll dough out on board, size 8 x 10 inches, then start to roll up like a jelly roll towards you. Press down on ends and edges to seal. Place in pans, let rise till pans are full. Bake at 375° for 45 minutes. Cool on rack. Oil top of loaves.

I have won many Blue ribbons on this recipe, also some special cash gifts and one diamond pin.

COMPRESSED YEAST BREAD

- 2 cups scalded milk, cooled
- 1 pkg. yeast
- 3 T melted shortening
- 4 T sugar
- 6 cups sifted flour
- 2 tsp. salt

Add sugar and yeast to cooled milk. When dissolved add 3 cups flour. Beat till smooth. Add shortening and salt, mix together. Add 3 more cups flour. Knead on floured board for about 10 minutes. Place in large greased bowl or pan. Put in warm place, covered. Let rise till double in bulk. Punch down and turn over. Let rise again. Divide in half, shape into loaves, place in greased pans, 9 x 4 x 3. Let rise until pans are full and rounded. Bake at 375° for 45 minutes. Cool on rack, brush tops with margarine.

WHOLE WHEAT BREAD

First mixture:
- 1 cake or 1 pkg. dry yeast
- 1 1/2 cups warm water
- 3 1/2 cups white flour, sifted
- 2 tsp. salt

Second mixture:
- 1/2 cup hot water
- 1/2 cup brown sugar
- 1/3 cup dark molasses
- 3 T shortening

2 1/2 cups whole wheat flour

Dissolve yeast in 1 1/2 cups warm water. Add white flour and salt. Beat till smooth. Let rise in warm place till light. Combine 1/2 cup hot water, brown sugar, molasses and shortening. Cool till lukewarm and add first mixture. Add whole wheat flour and mix till smooth. Knead dough on floured board 7 - 10 minutes. Place in greased bowl and cover in warm place 85º - 90º for about 1 1/2 hours. Divide in half. Shape into two loaves. Place in greased pans. Grease dough on top. Let rise till pans are full and dough is rounded above pans. Bake at 350º for 45 minutes. Cool and store.

•|•

PARKER HOUSE ROLLS

- 2 1/2 cups scalded milk
- 1 pkg. yeast
- 1/3 cup butter or margarine
- 2 tsp. salt
- 4 T sugar
- 6 cups sifted flour

Dissolve yeast in cooled milk. Add sugar and 2 cups flour to yeast mixture, beat till smooth. Add salt, melted butter or margarine and mix in remainder of flour. Knead on board (dough will be quite soft, you may have to use a little more flour on the board). Put in greased container, let rise and punch down and let rise again. Keep in warm place near heat from stove. Makes rolls into different shapes — buns or dinner rolls and Parker House Rolls. Let rise till light and bake at 350º for 20 - 30 minutes.

I won with this recipe many times.

DANISH PASTRY

2 pkgs. of dry or cake yeast
1/2 cup warm water
1/2 tsp. salt
2 1/2 sticks margarine

2 eggs, beaten
3/4 cup scalded milk, cooled
1/2 cup sugar
4 1/2 cups flour, sifted

Dissolve yeast in 1/2 cup warm water. Cut each stick of margarine into 4 strips lengthwise, put on foil and refrigerate umtil ready to use. Beat eggs, add sugar, salt and milk and add to yeast mixture. Beat in flour with spoon. Knead on floured board for 5 minutes. Roll out dough in a 15 inch square. Place all of margarine on 1/2 of dough within 1 inch of edge. Fold the other half of dough over margarine and seal edges. Quickly roll out to 24 x 8 inches from short side, fold in thirds, repeat folding and rolling twice. If margarine comes through, sprinkle on flour. Refrigerate for 30 minutes. Repeat rolling and folding again. Take half of the dough to work with and leave the other half in the refrigerator. Shape into different kinds of sweet rolls, fill with fruit and nuts. Let rise till light. Bake at 375° - 400° for 20 - 30 minutes.

A good winner.

✦│✦

DINNER ROLLS

2/3 cup warm water
2 tsp. sugar
1 pkg. yeast
} Mix and let dissolve

1 cup canned evaporated milk
1 tsp. salt
2 beaten eggs

6 T margarine
4 T sugar
5 cups flour

Heat canned milk, add margarine, sugar and salt. Let cool. Add all other ingredients, and beat until smooth. Knead on board for five minutes. Let rise in greased bowl until double in bulk. Shape into rolls. Makes about 2 1/2 dozen. Let rise until light. Bake at 375° for 20 minutes.

CINNAMON ROLLS

2/3 cup warm water
1 package yeast } Stir and let dissolve
1 tsp. sugar

1 cup canned evaporated milk (scalded). Let cool.
6 T melted lard or margarine
1 tsp. salt   2 eggs, beaten
1/3 cup sugar   5 cups sifted flour

Combine all ingredients, beat till smooth. Knead for five minutes. Place in greased bowl. Cover and keep in warm place until dough rises, about 45 minutes. Punch down, divide into two parts. Roll out on floured board. Spread dough with softened butter, then sprinkle with 2 T sugar and 1 T cinnamon. Roll up tightly like a jelly roll. With pastry scissors, clip in about 1 inch pieces, or cut with a sharp knife. Put in greased pans about 1 1/2 inches deep. Grease tops with soft margarine. Shake more cinnamon and sugar over top. Let rise about 30 minutes. Bake at 350° for 20 - 30 minutes. Cool on racks.

•I•

REFRIGERATOR ROLLS

1 cake or 1 pkg. of yeast   1/2 cup warm water
3/4 cup scalded milk, cooled
6 T sugar
2 tsp. salt   } MIX TOGETHER
5 T shortening

1 egg, beaten   4 1/2 cups flour

Dissolve 1 cake, or pkg., of yeast in 1/2 cup warm water. Stir into cooled milk mixture. Add 1 beaten egg and 2 1/2 cups flour. Beat till smooth. Add last 2 cups of flour. Mix and knead on bread board with a little flour. Put in greased bowl and let rise. Punch down and cover tightly with a damp cloth. Put in refrigerator for a few hours. Make rolls when you need them. Bake at 375° for 25 - 30 minutes.

COFFEE CAKE

First mixture

- 3/4 cup scalded milk, cooled
- 1/4 tsp. salt
- 1 cup sifted flour
- 1 T sugar
- 1/2 yeast cake or 1/2 pkg. dry yeast

Mix the above together and let rise till light.

Second mixture

- 1/3 cup butter
- 1 egg, beaten
- 1/2 tsp. cinnamon
- 1/2 cup sugar
- 1 1/4 cups flour
- 1/4 tsp. nutmeg

Cream butter and sugar. Add egg. Sift dry ingredients and mix both mixtures together for 5 minutes. Let rise, stir down and pour in greased baking pan.

TOPPING:

- 1 1/2 T margarine
- 1/4 tsp. cinnamon
- 1/4 cup sugar (brown or white)
- 1/8 tsp. cloves

Cream the above ingredients and spread over top of cake. Let rise 15 minutes. Raisins may be added if desired. Bake at 350° for about 35 - 40 minutes.

ENGLISH TEA MUFFINS

1/4 cup milk	2 T shortening
3/4 tsp. salt	1 T sugar
1/4 cup warm water	1/2 pkg. of dry yeast
1 1/2 cups sifted flour	

Scald milk, add shortening, salt and sugar. Cool. Dissolve yeast in warm water, add to other ingredients. Add flour. Mix well and knead on board. Roll out about 1/3 inch thick, cut with biscuit cutter. Place on cookie sheet sprinkled with corn meal. Let rise for 1 hour or till doubled in bulk. Bake on medium griddle, with corn meal sprinkled on griddle, about 7 minutes on each side.

I won with this recipe in 1973, and 1975 at the Illinois State Fair.

♦|♦

RYE BREAD

Soften 1 pkg. yeast in 1/2 cup warm water. Set aside. Combine in sauce pan, 1 cup sour milk, 1/3 cup brown sugar, 1/4 cup molasses, 2 tsp. salt, heat and bring to a boil, then cool. To this mixture, add 1/2 tsp. soda, 1/2 cup cold water, and 1/4 cup shortening. Stir together. Add yeast. Gradually add 3 cups of rye flour and 3 cups white flour. Let rise till double in a covered greased bowl. Punch down and let rise 30 minutes. Shape into 2 loaves and put into loaf bread pans, let rise till light. Bake at 350° 45 - 50 minutes.

QUICK BREADS

QUICK BREADS

BEST EVER BANANA BREAD

1 cup sugar	1/2 cup margarine
2 eggs, beaten	1 cup mashed bananas
1/4 cup sour milk	2 cups sifted flour
1/2 tsp. salt	1 tsp. soda
1/2 cup nuts, chopped	

Cream sugar and margarine. Add eggs and bananas. Add sifted dry ingredients alternately with milk. Add nuts. Bake in 8 x 4 x 3 greased pan at 325° - 350° for one hour. When cold, wrap in foil and keep in refrigerator.

Very good, also a good winner at State Fairs.

•|•

STEAMED BOSTON BROWN BREAD

2 1/2 cups graham flour	1 cup white flour
1/2 cup corn meal	1 cup molasses
3 tsp. soda	2 1/2 cups sour milk
1 tsp. salt	

Put soda in sour milk and mix all ingredients together. Put mixture in cans with lids which have been well greased. Fill about 2/3 full of batter. Put cans on a rack in a deep kettle. Keep water up several inches. Steam for 2 or 3 hours (depends how large the cans are). I put raisins in the batter, but the recipe doesn't call for them.

A good old recipe handed down. I have won on it several times.

NUT BREAD

2 cups flour, sifted	3 tsp. baking powder
3/4 tsp. salt	2 small eggs
5 T shortening	3/4 cup sugar
1 cup milk	1 cup chopped nuts

Cream shortening and sugar. Add beaten eggs. Add dry ingredients alternately with milk. Stir *lightly*. Bake in 1 pound loaf pan, which has been greased and floured, at 325º - 350º for one hour. Glaze the top with a little beaten whole egg; return to oven for 5 to 10 minutes.

I won another Blue Ribbon at the Illinois State Fair in 1975 on this Nut Bread recipe.

◆I◆

BRAN MUFFINS

1/2 cup all bran cereal	
1/2 cup boiling water	Mix gently
1/4 cup chopped dates	
1/4 cup seeded raisins	
1/2 cup shortening	1/2 cup wheat chex
1/2 cup sugar	1 1/4 cups flour
1 egg, beaten	1/2 tsp. salt
1 1/4 tsp. soda	
1 cup buttermilk	

Pour boiling water over bran and add dates and raisins. Set aside. Cream shortening and sugar, add egg. Add wheat cereal, flour, soda and salt alternately with buttermilk. Then add first mixture gently. Bake in greased muffin pans at 375º about 20 minutes, or until done.

CORN MUFFINS

1 cup sour milk
1/2 tsp. soda
3/4 cup yellow corn meal
2 tsp. baking powder
1 T sugar

1 egg
1 tsp. salt
1/2 cup flour
1 T melted lard or margarine

Put sour milk and egg in mixing bowl and beat well. Add soda and beat some more. Add other dry ingredients all at once and mix only lightly. Add lard or margarine and stir in. Heat muffin pans with a little lard or margarine in them. Fill 2/3 full. Bake at 425° for 15 - 20 minutes.

•|•

GRAHAM MUFFINS

1/2 cup graham flour
1/2 cup white flour
1 1/2 tsp. baking powder
1/2 tsp. salt
1 T sugar
} MIX TOGETHER

1 egg, beaten
1/2 cup sour milk
1 1/2 T melted lard or shortening
1/4 tsp. soda
} MIX TOGETHER

Mix all wet ingredients together. Add to dry ingredients and stir lightly. Fill greased muffin tins, about 2/3 full. Bake in a 425° oven about 20 minutes.

QUICK COFFEE CAKE

1/4 cup margarine 1/2 cup sugar
1 egg 1/2 tsp. salt
2 cups flour 3 tsp. baking powder
1/2 tsp. nutmeg 1/2 tsp. cinnamon
1 cup milk

Cream margarine and sugar together, beat egg and add. Sift flour, baking powder, and spices. Add alternately with milk, stir lightly,

TOPPING:

1/2 cup graham cracker crumbs 2 T margarine
2 T sugar 1/4 tsp. cinnamon
1/8 tsp. cloves

Mix together and spread on top and bake at 400° for 40 - 45 minutes in 8 x 8 x 2 pan.

RAISED DOUGHNUTS

> 3/4 cup milk
> 1 T sugar   } Heat and let cool
> 1/4 tsp. salt

Add:
> 1 pkg. yeast (to above mixture)
> 1 cup flour

Beat till smooth. Let rise 30 minutes.

Add:

> 1/3 cup margarine
> 1/2 cup sugar   } Creamed together

> 1 egg, beaten   1 tsp. vanilla
> 1 1/2 cups sifted flour 1/4 tsp nutmeg

Add all to first mixture. Beat together for 5 minutes. Let rise 30 minutes. Roll out on floured board 1/2 inch thick. Cut with biscuit cutter. Let rise on floured cookie sheet. Fry in deep hot fat or corn oil. Drain on paper toweling. Dust with sugar or dip in glaze.

GLAZE:

Soak 1/2 package of unflavored gelatin in 2 cups warm water ($150°$). Add 5 pounds powdered sugar, a dash of salt and 1 tsp. Vanilla. Heat stirring constantly, until dissolved into hot clear syrup, but do not boil. Dip cooled doughnuts into hot icing. Let drain on rack.

CHEESE STICKS

1 1/2 T butter	1/4 tsp. salt
1/2 cup grated cheese	1/2 cup flour
2 T ice water	dash of cayenne pepper

Mix butter and cheese evenly through flour. Add water and pepper. Roll out the thickness of pie crust. Cut strips 1 inch wide by 4-5 inches long. Bake on cookie sheets at 375° for 5 to 10 minutes.

Very good. A prize winner every time I entered them at the Fair.

COOKIES and BARS

COOKIES AND BARS

GERMAN FRUIT COOKIES

1/2 cup shortening
1/2 cup brown sugar
1/2 cup granulated sugar
1/4 tsp. salt
1 tsp. soda
} CREAM TOGETHER WITH MIXER

Add:
1 egg, beaten
1 tsp. vanilla

Add:
1 2/3 cups flour, sifted
1/4 tsp. cinnamon
1/4 tsp. nutmeg
} SIFT TOGETHER

Add:
1/2 cup mixed candied fruit & peel
1/2 cup dates, chopped
1/2 cup candied cherries, chopped
1/2 cup raisins
1/2 cup nuts, chopped
} MIX TOGETHER AND ADD 1 T FLOUR TO COAT THE FRUIT

Mix all together, refrigerate overnight. Shape into small balls and press flat, add 1/2 cherry on top. Bake at 350° for 20 minutes on a greased cookie sheet.

These German Fruit Cookies were a big winner in 1969 and were judged the best cookie of the show. I won a special prize of a $100 bond. In 1970 and 1971, 1972, 1973, 1974 and 1975, they won first in their class.

GINGER COOKIES (FROSTED)

3 cups sifted flour	1 tsp. ginger
1/2 cup shortening	1/2 cup sugar
1/2 tsp. salt	1 cup molasses
1/3 cup sour milk	1 1/2 tsp. soda
1 egg	

Cream shortening and sugar. Cream in molasses. Beat in egg. Add soda to sour milk, Add salt and ginger to flour. Add flour alternately with sour milk. Mix till smooth. Chill dough several hours. Roll out on floured board. Cut with biscuit cutter. Bake on greased cookie sheet in preheated 350° oven for 10 - 15 minutes. For frosted cremes, ice with Powdered Sugar Icing or Seven Minute Icing.

Good old time molasses ginger cookie, also a prize winner.

✦|✦

PEANUT BUTTER COOKIES

1/2 cup shortening	1/2 cup peanut butter
1/2 cup granulated sugar	1/2 cup brown sugar
1 egg	1 1/2 cups flour
1/2 tsp. baking powder	3/4 tsp. soda
1/4 tsp. salt	

Cream shortening, peanut butter and sugars. Beat in egg. Sift all dry ingredients. Add to first mixture. Shape into small balls and press them flat on cookie sheet with fork dipped in flour. Bake at 350° 10-15 minutes.

Another good Fair winner.

BOILED RAISIN COOKIES

1 cup shortening	2 cups sugar
1 1/2 tsp. salt	1 tsp. soda
1 cup water	2 cups raisins
3 eggs	1 tsp. vanilla
3 3/4 cups flour, sifted	1 tsp. baking powder
1/2 tsp. cinnamon	1/4 tsp. nutmeg
1 cup chopped nuts	

Add water to raisins, heat and boil for 5 minutes. Drain and reserve 1/2 cup liquid. Stir soda in raisins, after draining. Cream shortening with sugar. Beat in eggs, one at a time. Sift flour, baking powder, spices and salt. Add with 1/2 cup liquid from raisins. Add raisins and nuts. Drop by spoonfuls on greased and floured cookie sheet. Bake at 350° 10 - 15 minutes.

Hope you try this one as it is a good and moist cookie.

•I•

TIGER COOKIES

1 1/2 cups crushed sugar coated corn flakes	
1 cup and 1 T sifted flour	1/4 tsp. salt
1/4 tsp. soda	1/2 cup corn oil margarine
1/2 tsp. vanilla	1/2 cup sugar
1 egg	1/2 pkg. (or 1/2 cup) choc. chips, melted

Measure crushed corn flakes, and set aside. Measure flour and set aside. Cream together margarine, salt, soda and sugar. Add egg and vanilla, beat well. Add dry ingredients. Stir in corn flakes Swirl in melted chocolate, stir lightly, leaving chocolate in streaks. Drop by spoonfuls on greased cookie sheet. Bake at 375° about 12 minutes.

ICE BOX COOKIES

1/2 cup butter	1 cup medium brown sugar
1 egg	1 2/3 cups flour
1/2 tsp. cream of tartar	1/3 tsp. soda
1/2 tsp. vanilla	1/2 cup nuts, chopped

Cream the butter and sugar. Beat in egg. Add dry ingredients. Add nuts last. Mold in 2 rolls and wrap in waxed paper. Chill over night, or to get it firmer, put in freezer awhile. Slice in 1/4 inch slices. Bake on teflon cookie sheets at 375° for 10 - 15 minutes.

Try this one, I like it, I hope you do. It won first at the Illinois State Fair in 1975.

♦I♦

CHOCOLATE ICE BOX COOKIES

3/4 cup shortening
3/4 cup granulated sugar   ⎫
3/4 cup brown sugar   ⎬ CREAM TOGETHER WITH MIXER
1/2 tsp. salt   ⎪
1/2 tsp. soda   ⎭

1 3/4 cups flour, sifted	1 tsp. baking powder
1 tsp. vanilla	2/3 cup chopped nuts
1 egg, unbeaten	2 oz. of baking chocolate, melted

Beat in egg with first mixture. Add melted chocolate, vanilla, and dry ingredients. Add nuts last. Mold in two rolls and wrap in waxed paper and chill for several hours in refrigerator. Cut into 1/4 inch slices using a sharp knife. Bake on greased cookie sheet at 375° for 10 - 15 minutes.

If you like chocolate, you will like this one. It is also a prize winner.

MOTHER'S BEST OATMEAL COOKIES

1/2 cup shortening
1/2 cup granulated sugar
1/2 cup light brown sugar   } CREAM TOGETHER
1/2 tsp. soda
1/2 tsp. salt
1 tsp. vanilla

1 tsp. baking powder
1 egg
1 cup and 1 T flour

1 T milk
1 cup quick, dry oats

Add egg to creamed mixture and beat. Add flour and baking powder, and 1 T milk. Add quick dry oats last. Drop by teaspoon on greased and floured cookie sheet. Bake at 375° – 10 - 15 minutes. You may add raisins and/or nuts, if desired.

This is another good winner.

•|•

SUGAR DROPS

1/2 cup margarine
1/2 cup corn oil
1/2 cup granulated sugar
1/2 cup powdered sugar
1/2 tsp. vanilla

1 egg, beaten
1/2 tsp. soda
2 cups flour
1/2 tsp. cream of tartar
1/2 tsp. salt

Cream corn oil, margarine, and both sugars. Add vanilla, egg and soda. Sift flour, cream of tartar and salt. Stir in and blend. Roll teaspoon of dough into a ball and press flat on a greased cookie sheet. Sprinkle sugar on top. Bake at 375° for 12 - 15 minutes.

Another good cookie, also a Blue Ribbon winner in 1975.

OATMEAL DATE COOKIES

1 cup brown sugar	1/2 cup margarine
1/4 tsp. salt	2 eggs, beaten
2 cups flour	1/4 tsp. cinnamon
1/8 tsp. cloves	1/8 tsp. nutmeg
1/2 tsp. soda	1/2 cup sour milk
1 cup quick, dry oats	1 cup dates, cut fine
1 tsp. baking powder	

Cream margarine and sugar. Combine soda and sour milk. Combine baking powder with flour. Add eggs to creamed mixture. Sift spices with flour, and add alternately with sour milk. Add oats and dates last. Drop by spoonfuls on greased cookie sheet. Bake at 375° for 10 - 15 minutes.

COCONUT MACAROONS

1 large egg white	1/4 tsp. cream of tartar
pinch of salt	1/2 cup powdered sugar
1/4 tsp. vanilla	enough flaked coconut to make batter stiff (about 2 cups)

Beat egg white until foamy. Add salt and cream of tartar and beat until stiff. Add sugar and beat very stiff. Stir in coconut. Drop by spoonfuls on teflon cookie sheet. Bake at 300° - 325° for 10 - 15 minutes.

Another good winner. It won first prize in 1975 at the Illinois State Fair.

CHOCOLATE RAISIN COOKIES

2 1/2 cups sugar
2 eggs, beaten
4 cups flour, sifted
4 squares chocolate, melted
2 cups raisins
1 cup nuts

1 cup shortening (room temperature)
1 cup milk
4 tsp. baking powder
1 tsp. salt
2 tsp. vanilla

Cream shortening and sugar. Add beaten eggs, vanilla and chocolate. Add dry ingredients with milk. Stir in raisins and nuts last. Drop by teaspoon on greased baking sheets. Bake at 350° for 10 - 15 minutes.

A good chocolaty drop cookie.

♦│♦

KISSES

3 egg whites
pinch of salt
2 cups powdered sugar

1/3 tsp. cream of tartar
1/2 tsp. vanilla

Beat egg whites till foamy, add cream of tartar and salt. Continue beating till very stiff. Add sugar and vanilla. Beat till it will stand in high peaks. Drop by teaspoon on ungreased cookie sheet, teflon coated. Bake at 275° - 300° for 20 minutes, or longer, till done on the inside.

A good winner several times.

OAT KRISPIES

1/2 cup shortening	1/2 cup brown sugar
1/2 tsp. salt	1/2 cup granulated sugar
1 egg	1 cup flour
1 1/4 cups quick, dry oats	1/2 tsp. soda
1/4 cup nuts, chopped	1/2 tsp. vanilla

Cream shortening and sugars with soda, salt and vanilla, beat in egg. Add flour, oats and nuts. Make in a roll, wrap in foil, chill over night. Slice and bake at 375° for 10 - 15 minutes on a greased cookie sheet.

Try this one, I think you will like them.

♦I♦

CHOCOLATE KRINKLE COOKIES

1/2 cup shortening	1/2 cup brown sugar
1/2 cup granulated sugar	1 egg, beaten
1 1/3 cups flour, sifted	1/2 tsp. salt
1/2 tsp. soda	1/2 tsp. vanilla
1/2 pkg. chocolate chips, melted	

Cream shortening with sugars. Add beaten egg, salt, vanilla, soda, and chocolate. Add flour. Drop on greased cookie sheet. Bake at 350° for 10 - 15 minutes.

FILLED COOKIES

1/2 cup light brown sugar
1/4 cup plus 1 T margarine
1/2 tsp. vanilla
1 tsp. baking powder

2 T granulated sugar
1 egg, beaten
1 1/4 cups flour
1/4 tsp. soda

FILLING:

3/4 cup dates, chopped
1/4 cup water

2 T sugar
1 T lemon juice

Cook all filling ingredients together and cool. Cream sugars and margarine, add egg and rest of ingredients and mix well. Roll dough thin as pie dough. Cut with cookie cutter. Put 1 tsp. filling on one circle, lay another one over top and press edges together with a fork. Bake at 350° for 20 minutes.

Another first prize winner at the Illinois State Fair, 1975.

•I•

MOTHER'S SUGAR COOKIES

1 cup butter
2/3 tsp. soda
3 eggs, beaten
3 2/3 cups sifted flour

2 cups sugar
1 tsp. vanilla
1/2 tsp. salt
2 tsp. baking powder

Cream butter and sugar with soda, salt and vanilla. Add beaten eggs. Sift flour and baking powder. Add to creamed mixture. Chill dough till firm enough to roll out on floured pastry cloth. Roll a little sugar in on top of dough. Cut with biscuit cutter or other fancy shapes. Bake at 425° till brown, on a greased and floured cookie sheet, or one teflon coated is best.

This recipe is very old. Do not add any liquid other than the eggs. I have won with it many times.

PINWHEEL COOKIES

1/2 cup margarine	1/2 cup granulated sugar
1/2 cup brown sugar	1/2 tsp. salt
1/2 tsp. soda	1/2 tsp. vanilla
1 egg, beaten	1 3/4 cups sifted flour

Blend soda, salt and vanilla with shortening and sugar, cream together. Beat in egg. Add flour last, chill dough 30 - 40 minutes.

FILLING:

1/2 lb. dates, cut up	1/4 cup sugar
1/4 cup water	2 T orange marmalade

Cook dates, sugar and water until a thick paste, add marmalade and cool. Roll out dough like pie dough, spread filling over top. Roll up like jelly roll. Wrap in foil or wax paper and chill over night. Slice with a sharp knife and place on cookie sheet. Bake at 350° for 10 - 15 minutes.

A State Fair winner.

CLOUD NINE BUTTERSCOTCH BARS

1/2 cup margarine	2 eggs, beaten
1 pkg. instant butterscotch pudding	1 tsp. vanilla
	1 tsp. baking powder
1 cup flour, sifted	1 cup quick, dry oats
1/2 cup milk	1 cup chocolate chips

Beat margarine till creamy. Add dry pudding, eggs, vanilla. Add flour with baking powder alternately with milk. Beat well by hand, stir in oats and chocolate chips. Spread batter in greased 9 x 9 x 2 pan. Bake at 350° for 20 - 25 minutes. Ice with chocolate frosting and cut in bars.

FROSTING:

2 T thin cream	2 T margarine
1/2 cup chocolate chips, melted	enough powdered sugar to thicken

Heat cream and margarine. Beat in enough powdered sugar to thicken and about 1/2 cup melted chocolate chips. Spread on top and cut in bars.

•I•

DATE NUT BARS

1/2 cup sugar	
1/2 cup flour, unsifted	1/4 cup margarine
2 eggs	1/2 tsp. baking powder
1/4 tsp. salt	1 1/2 cups chopped dates
3/4 cup chopped nuts	1 tsp. vanilla

Cream margarine and sugar. Add egg yolks. Add dry ingredients, dates and nuts. Add beaten egg whites last. Mix well. Pour in 6 x 10 inch pan (well greased). Bake at 275° - 300° about 45 minutes.

I won with this one many, many times.

APPLE WALNUT SQUARES

1/4 cup margarine	1 cup sifted flour
1/2 cup sugar	1 tsp. baking powder
1 egg, beaten	1/2 tsp. soda
1/2 tsp. vanilla	1/4 tsp. salt
1 T water	1/4 tsp. cinnamon
1/2 cup nuts, chopped	1/8 tsp. nutmeg
1 large apple, peeled & diced	1/3 cup canned, evaporated milk

Cream margarine and sugar, add egg, vanilla and water. Add all dry ingredients and evaporated milk and mix well. Fold in apple and nuts. Pour into greased 9 inch pan. Bake at 350° for 30 minutes. Cool slightly.

ICING:

1 cup powdered sugar	1 T margarine
2 T milk	dash of salt

Heat milk and margarine, add sugar and beat. Ice, and cut in squares.

Very good.

•I•

SOUR MILK DOUGHNUTS

2 eggs, beaten	1 cup sugar
1 cup sour milk	1/2 tsp. salt
1/2 tsp. soda	2 tsp. baking powder
3 T melted margarine	3 3/4 cups flour (about)
3/4 tsp. vanilla	

Mix all ingredients together. Chill batter several hours. Fry in deep, hot fat (or you can fry each day just what you need that day). Roll in granulated sugar. The batter will keep in refrigerator for several days. If the batter is very cold, it can be rolled and cut with biscuit cutter. Or, it may be dropped from a spoon in the hot fat and fried.

CAKES

CAKES

COCONUT WHITE CAKE

2/3 cup shortening (about 2 T of it creamery butter for flavor)
1/2 tsp. salt   2 cups fine sugar
3 cups and 3 T sifted cake flour 1 1/4 cups milk
3 tsp. baking powder   4 large egg whites
1 tsp. vanilla   coconut

Cream shortening and sugar, salt and vanilla till creamy. Add flour and milk alternately. Add baking powder to last portion of flour. Add beaten egg whites, fold in *lightly*. Bake in two 8 inch greased and lightly floured pans, with wax paper, at 300° for about 1 hour. This is a very rich cake so bake slowly. Ice when cold with Seven Minute Icing, (recipe found on page 55). Sprinkle with plenty of coconut.

This cake is the Queen of them all. I have won 5 trophies on it as Best of Show, 1960, 1966, 1969, 1970, 1974. In 1971, 1972, 1973, 1975, I won Blue Ribbons for Best in its Class.

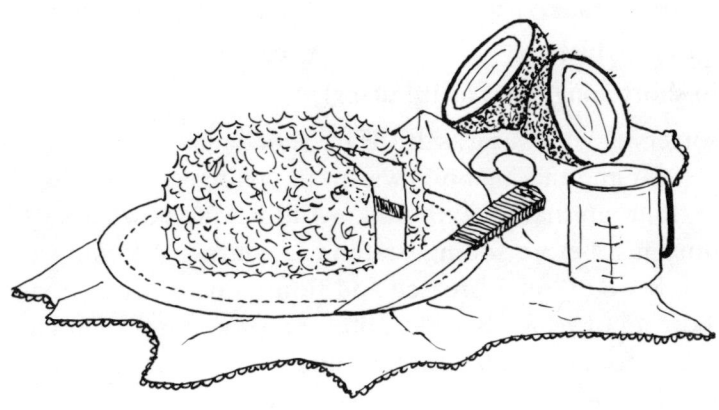

BURNT SUGAR CAKE

1/2 cup sugar	1/2 cup hot water
1/2 cup shortening	1 1/2 cups sugar
2 egg yolks	1/2 tsp. soda
1/2 tsp. salt	3 cups cake flour, sifted
3 tsp. baking powder	1 tsp. vanilla
7/8 cup water	2 egg whites

Burn 1/2 cup sugar in a skillet over low heat till melted and it bubbles up and smells like molasses. Add hot water. You will have about 1/2 cup syrup. Let it cool. Cream shortening and sugar, add burnt sugar syrup. Beat in egg yolks. Add dry ingredients (sifted together). Add water. Beat 2 egg whites and add last. Bake in two eight inch pans at 350° for 40 - 50 minutes. Ice with Caramel Icing.

They say, "Why burn the sugar?" but this too, has won many times!

◆I◆

HICKORY NUT CAKE

2 cups sugar	1/2 tsp. salt
1 tsp. vanilla	1 1/4 cups milk
3 cups cake flour, sifted	3 tsp. baking powder
4 large egg whites	1 cup hickory nuts, chopped
2/3 cup shortening (part of it butter)	

Cream shortening with sugar, salt. Have shortening warm and soft. Also have sugar and mixing bowl warm, to cream easy and fluffy. Add some flour alternately with milk. Add baking powder with a little of flour just before adding beaten egg whites. Add nuts last. Bake in two 8 x 8 x 2 inch greased and floured pans, with waxed paper in bottom of pans. Bake at 300° for 30 minutes then increase to about 325° for about 30 minutes more. If you cannot get hickory nuts, other chopped nuts may be substituted.

Hope you try this one sometime. Best of all nut cakes.

DEVIL'S FOOD CAKE

1/2 cup shortening	1 tsp. soda
1 1/2 cups sugar	1 tsp. vanilla
2 egg yolks	1/2 tsp. salt
2 cups cake flour	1 cup cold water
1 tsp. baking powder	2 oz. or squares of baking chocolate, melted
2 egg whites	

Cream together shortening and sugar. Add soda, vanilla and salt. Beat in egg yolks, add chocolate to mixture. Add baking powder, flour and cold water alternately to the batter. Beat egg whites and fold in last. Bake in two 8 or 9 inch pans at 350° for 45 - 50 minutes. Ice with any kind of icing.

A rich delicious cake. It has won several Blue Ribbons.

•I•

JELLY ROLL

6 egg yolks	1/2 cup hot water
1 cup sugar	1 1/2 cups cake flour, sifted
1/2 tsp. salt	1 tsp. vanilla
2 tsp. baking powder	

Beat egg yolks till light, add sugar and beat. Add hot water, beat. Add dry ingredients and vanilla and beat 2 minutes. Pour in large shallow pan. Better to use teflon coated pan. Bake at 350° for about 30 minutes. Take out of pan at once onto a damp cloth. Cut off crust edges, spread with jelly, roll up, wrap cloth around it for about 20 minutes, then loosen. Sprinkle top with powdered sugar before serving.

LEMON YELLOW CAKE

3/4 cup butter
1 cup milk
3 cups cake flour, sifted
1/2 tsp. salt
4 egg whites

2 cups sugar
4 egg yolks
3 tsp. baking powder
1 tsp. lemon extract

Cream butter and sugar well with an electric mixer. Add egg yolks 2 at a time and beat well. Sift dry ingredients and add alternately with milk and flavoring. Fold in beaten egg whites last. Bake in two 8 inch layer pans for about 30 minutes at $325°$ - $350°$. Good with lemon filling between the layers and powdered sugar icing on top and sides of cake.

LEMON FILLING:

3/4 cup sugar
1/16 tsp. salt
1 tsp. grated lemon rind
2 or 3 egg yolks

3 T flour
1/4 cup lemon juice
1/2 cup water
2 T butter

Mix all together and cook in double boiler. Cook till thick (about 15 minutes). Cool and spread between layers.

A good winner at the Illinois State Fair several times.

- 38 -

KENTUCKY CREAM CAKE

1 stick margarine	2 1/4 cups all purpose flour
1/2 cup vegetable shortening	1 tsp. soda
2 cups sugar	1 cup buttermilk
5 egg yolks	1 tsp. vanilla
5 egg whites, beaten	1 cup coconut
2/3 cup chopped nuts	

Cream shortening and margarine with sugar. Add egg yolks one at a time. Beat well. Add dry ingredients alternately with buttermilk. Add vanilla, coconut and nuts. Lastly fold in beaten egg whites. Bake in two or three layers 8 x 8 x 2 at 350° about 35 - 40 minutes.

FROSTING:

1 - 8 oz. pkg. cream cheese	1/2 stick margarine
1 - box (1 lb) powdered sugar	1 tsp. vanilla

Cream all together. Frost cake. Put chopped nuts on top of cake.

Very good!

•I•

APPLESAUCE CAKE I

1/2 cup shortening	1 3/4 cups sugar
1 egg	1 1/2 cups applesauce, unsweetened
1/2 tsp. cinnamon	
2 1/2 cups flour, sifted	1/4 tsp. salt
1/4 tsp. nutmeg	1/4 tsp. cloves
1/2 cup chopped nuts	1 1/2 tsp. soda
1/2 cup boiling water	1 cup chopped raisins

Cream shortening and sugar. Add well beaten egg. Add cold applesauce. Add dry ingredients with hot water, with soda dissolved in water. Fold in nuts and raisins last. Pour in greased and floured pan, size 8 x 12 x 2. Bake at 350° for 1 hour.

APPLESAUCE CAKE II

1/2 cup shortening, part margarine	1 cup brown sugar, packed
2 eggs well beaten	2 cups cake flour
1/4 tsp. salt	2/3 tsp. cinnamon
1/4 tsp. cloves	2/3 tsp. nutmeg
1 tsp. soda	1/2 cup nuts, chopped
1 cup applesauce	1/2 cup raisins, if desired

Cream shortening and sugar. Add beaten eggs. Add dry ingredients alternately with applesauce. Bake in 9 inch square pan at 325° - 350° for 1 hour.

State Fair Blue Ribbon winner 1973, 1974, 1975. This is a newer recipe, and I have won a Blue Ribbon with it at the Illinois State Fair the last 3 years.

•I•

CHOCOLATE ANGEL FOOD CAKE

2 cups egg whites	2 tsp. cream of tartar
1/2 tsp. salt	2 1/4 cups sugar
1/3 cup cocoa (sifted in part of sugar)	
1 1/8 cups cake flour	1 tsp. vanilla

Beat egg whites till foamy, then add salt, cream of tartar and vanilla. Beat to soft peaks with electric mixer. Fold in (by hand) 1/3 of the sugar, sift 1/2 of the sugar with cocoa and fold in gently. Add rest of sugar to flour. Fold in very *lightly*. Bake in large tube pan at 300° for 15 minutes, then at 325° for 45 minutes. Cool in inverted pan. Loosen edges with a knife and remove cooled cake. Ice with Seven Minute Icing.

ANGEL FOOD CAKE

1 1/2 cups cake flour, sifted	2 1/4 cups sifted sugar
2 tsp. cream of tartar	1/2 tsp. orange extract
1/2 tsp. salt	1 tsp. vanilla
1/4 tsp. almond extract	2 cups egg whites

Sift cake flour 4 times, then add 3/4 cup sugar and sift 4 more times, and set aside. Beat egg whites in large mixer bowl till foamy. Add salt, flavoring and cream of tartar. Continue beating until stiff enough to stand in soft peaks. Beat at slow speed, adding sugar 2 T at a time. Remove bowl from mixer. Add the flour and sugar mixture in 6 portions by hand. Fold in with flat wire beater, very lightly until smooth. Pour in large tube cake pan. Bake at $325°$ for first 30 minutes, then $350°$ for the last 25 - 30 minutes. Invert in pan till cold. Loosen edges from the pan. Remove. Ice with Seven Minute Icing.

Very good, I have won Blue Ribbons on it.

◆I◆

PRUNE CAKE

Cook prunes in small amount of water. Cut up 1 cup of prunes. Set aside and cool.

1/2 cup vegetable shortening	2 1/2 cups all purpose flour
1 1/2 cups sugar	1 tsp. baking powder
3 eggs, beaten	1 tsp. soda (put in the milk)
1 cup sour milk	1/3 tsp. cinnamon
1/2 tsp. salt	1/8 tsp. cloves
1 cup prunes	

Cream shortening and sugar till creamy. Beat in eggs, one at a time. Mix in flour, spices and baking powder alternately with sour milk. Add prunes last. Bake in two 8 x 8 x 2 inch pans at $325°$ - $350°$ for about 35 - 40 minutes. Cool on rack. Ice with Caramel Icing.

PINEAPPLE UPSIDE DOWN CAKE

2/3 cup brown sugar
pineapple rings
walnut halves

3 T margarine
maraschino cherries

Melt margarine in 10 inch round pan or 9 x 9 x 2 inch square pan. Sprinkle in brown sugar. Over this, place pineapple rings with maraschino cherries and walnut halves. Heat oven to 350°. Have pan hot to put the batter in.

3 eggs
1 3/4 cups cake flour, sifted
1/2 tsp. salt
1/2 tsp. baking powder

1 cup granulated sugar
1/2 cup syrup from pineapple
1 tsp. vanilla

Beat eggs until light and fluffy. Beat sugar in gradually. Add syrup. Sift flour, salt and baking powder. Add all at once and beat with spoon until smooth. Pour over pineapple-sugar mixture. Bake at 350° for 50 - 60 minutes, or till cake is done. Turn out on large plate. Serve warm with whipped topping.

Hope you try this. I won first prize at the State Fair in 1974, 1975.

♦I♦

MY MOTHER'S SOFT GINGERBREAD

1 1/2 cups molasses
1/2 cup sour milk
1 1/2 tsp. soda
3 1/2 cups flour

1/2 cup butter or lard
2 eggs, well beaten
1 T ginger

Stir shortening, molasses and ginger together. Add milk and eggs. Dissolve soda in a little hot water, add it, and flour. Bake at 325° for 15 - 20 minutes.

Quite an old recipe.

CHOCOLATE MARSHMALLOW ROLL

2/3 cup cake flour, sifted	1/4 tsp. salt
3/4 cup sugar	4 eggs, separated
1 tsp. vanilla	3 T cocoa
1/2 tsp. baking powder	1/4 tsp. soda

1 square baking chocolate (unsweetened), melted

Sift cocoa, salt, baking powder and soda. Beat egg yolks till thick, add part of sugar. Beat egg whites till stiff, add part of sugar. Fold yolk mixture and white mixture together. Add dry ingredients. Add vanilla and chocolate last. Bake in 15 x 10 x 1-1/2 greased and floured pan, at 375° - 400° for 15 - 20 minutes. Remove from pan onto dry cloth. Roll up cloth with cake and leave till cold. Unroll and spread with the following prepared icing.

ICING:

3 T water	1 large egg white
dash of salt	1/4 tsp. cream of tartar
3/4 cup sugar	1 tsp. plain gelatin
1 T water	chocolate chips

Mix in double boiler, 3 T water, egg white, salt, cream of tartar, and sugar. Cook over hot water about 5 minutes, *beating constantly* with electric mixer. Have prepared 1 tsp. plain gelatin, dissolved in 1 T water. Beat into above mixture, cool and spread on cake. Re-roll tight with cloth around outside. Ice roll on outside with melted chocolate chips if desired.

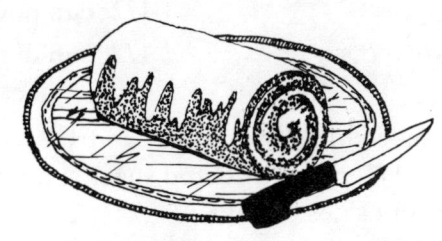

PINEAPPLE CHIFFON CAKE

Step One:

- 2 cups sifted cake flour
- 3 tsp. baking powder
- 1 1/2 cups sugar
- 1 tsp. salt

Sift together into bowl.

Make a well in dry ingredients and add in order:

- 1/2 cup cooking oil
- 7 unbeaten egg yolks
- 3/4 cup pineapple juice
- 2 tsp. grated lemon rind
- 1 1/2 tsp. vanilla
- 1/2 cup drained pineapple

Beat with a spoon until smooth.

Step Two:

Measure in large mixing bowl:

- 1 cup egg whites (7 or 8)
- 1/2 tsp. cream of tartar

Beat until egg whites form very stiff peaks.

Step Three:

Pour first mixture over whipped egg whites. Gently fold by hand just until blended. *Do Not Stir.* Pour into ungreased tube pan 10 x 4 inches. Bake at 325º for 50 - 55 minutes. Cool in pan upside down. Loosen edges and remove. Ice with Creamy Pineapple Icing.

CREAMY PINEAPPLE ICING:

- 2 T shortening
- 1/4 tsp. salt
- 2 1/2 cups powdered sugar
- 1 T butter
- 1/2 cup powdered sugar
- 1/2 cup drained, crushed pineapple

Cream together shortening, butter, salt and 1/2 cup powdered sugar. Add alternately 2 1/2 cups powdered sugar and pineapple. Beat till creamy. Ice top and sides of cake.

Very delicious.

ORANGE CANDY SURPRISE CAKE (Original)

1 pkg. lemon cake mix (19 oz. size)	1 3 oz. pkg. instant vanilla pudding
4 eggs	3/4 cup milk
1/2 cup corn oil	2 bananas, peeled and cut in chunks
1/2 tsp. almond extract	
8 oz. orange candy slices, (cut in pieces)	1 cup flaked coconut

In large mixing bowl, combine all ingredients except orange candy. Stir to blend, then beat at medium speed for 5 minutes. Lightly stir in orange candy. Pour in oblong pan 8 x 12 x 2, well greased with heavy waxed paper in bottom of pan. Bake at 325° for 70 - 80 minutes, or until done.

GLAZE FOR TOP OF CAKE:

1/4 cup orange juice	1/4 cup lemon juice
3/4 cup powdered sugar	1 tsp. grated orange peel
1 tsp. grated lemon peel	coconut

Heat all until thick and syrupy. Pour on cake while warm and sprinkle coconut over top. When cool remove cake from pan.

GLAZE FOR SIDES OF CAKE:

2 T warm water	2 T butter
enough powdered sugar to thicken	

Beat all of the above ingredients and ice sides of cake.

A big winner at the State Fair.

PINEAPPLE CAKE

1/2 cup shortening	1 1/3 cups sugar
2 1/2 cups sifted cake flour	2 1/2 tsp. baking powder
1/2 tsp. salt	3 egg whites, beaten
1/2 cup pineapple juice	1/2 cup water
1 tsp. vanilla	

Cream shortening with sugar. Add dry ingredients alternately with liquids and vanilla. Fold in beaten egg whites last. Bake in two 8" pans at $325°$ for 35 - 40 minutes. Cool on rack.

PINEAPPLE FILLING:

1/2 cup pineapple juice	3/4 cup crushed pineapple
3/4 cup sugar	1/4 tsp. salt
3 T cornstarch	1 T lemon juice
1 T butter	

Cook all ingredients except lemon juice and butter in double boiler, for about 15 minutes. Add lemon juice and butter last. Beat well. Cool before spreading between cake layers.

Ice top and sides with Seven Minute Icing.

LAZY DAISY CAKE

2 eggs	1 cup sugar
1/4 tsp. salt	2 tsp. baking powder
1 cup cake flour	1 tsp. vanilla
1/2 cup milk	1 T margarine

Beat eggs well, add dry ingredients. Heat milk with margarine. Add to other mixture and stir well. Bake 30 minutes at 350º.

TOPPING:

2 T butter	5 T brown sugar
2 T cream	1/2 cup coconut

Heat butter, sugar, and cream to a boil. Add coconut. Spread over cake and return to oven for 10 minutes.

A quickie. Easy to make. Very good.

•|•

CAKE OF THE GOLDEN WEST

1/2 cup shortening (part butter)	1 1/2 cups sugar
1/4 tsp. salt	1 cup milk
1 tsp. vanilla	2 1/2 cups cake flour, sifted
3 large egg whites	2 1/2 tsp. baking powder

Cream shortening, salt and vanilla with sugar till light and fluffy (use electric mixer, have shortening soft, but not melted, also sugar and bowl warm – helps to make it cream easier). Add flour alternately with milk. Add baking powder with last portion of flour. Add egg whites beaten stiff, last, and fold in lightly by hand. Bake in large 9 inch square pan, two inches deep, at 300º - 325º for 1 hour. Ice with any kind of icing, caramel or chocolate is good. Look for icing recipes included in this book.

Another good butter cake.

RAINBOW CAKETTES (Original)

1 cup miniature marshmallows (colored)	1 box white cake mix (19 oz. size)
1 1/2 cups cherry pie filling	1 box cherry jello
2 egg whites	1 1/2 cups water
1/2 tsp. almond extract	1/2 tsp. orange flavoring

Stir jello into pie cherries (cut up) and set aside. Grease muffin pans and dust with cornstarch. Place marshmallows evenly in bottom of pans (4 or 5 to each cup). Set aside. Put cake mix in large bowl. Add water, flavoring, and egg whites to cake mix. Beat at medium speed for 2 minutes. Spoon batter over marshmallows. Fill about 2/3 full. Then put a spoonful of cherry mixture on top of batter. Bake at 350º for 30 - 35 minutes. Cool for 15 minutes. Remove from pans top side up.

Try this one, I like it!

•I•

NEVER FAIL CUPCAKES

1 egg	1 tsp. vanilla
1/3 ~~1/2~~ cup cocoa	1 tsp. soda
1/2 cup shortening	1 cup sugar
1 1/2 cups flour	1/2 cup hot water
1/2 cup (large) sour milk	

Put these ingredients into a bowl, in the order they are given. Do not mix until the last of them has been added. Then beat well. Bake in a moderate oven in cupcake tins, at 350º for 15 - 20 minutes.

Very good. I am sure the kiddies will like these.

PINEAPPLE COCONUT CUPCAKES

1/2 cup flaked coconut	1/4 cup water
1/2 cup margarine	3/4 tsp. vanilla
1 cup crushed pineapple	1 cup sugar
2 eggs, unbeaten	2 cups flour
2 tsp. baking powder	1/2 tsp. salt

Combine coconut and water. Let stand while mixing the cake. Cream margarine, sugar, salt and vanilla. Add eggs one at a time and beat well. Add coconut. Mix well. Add dry ingredients and pineapple alternately and mix well. Bake in cupcake tins at 350° for 15 - 20 minutes.

FROSTING:

3 oz. cream cheese	2 1/2 cups confectioners sugar
1 T milk	1/4 tsp. vanilla
pinch of salt	

Mix all of the above ingredients together until smooth and ice cupcakes.

CARROT PINEAPPLE CAKE

1 1/2 cups corn oil	2 cups flour
2 cups sugar	2 cups grated carrots
4 eggs	1 tsp. cinnamon
1 small can crushed pineapple	2 tsp. baking powder
1 tsp. salt	1/2 tsp. soda
1 tsp. vanilla	1/2 cup nuts

Cream oil and sugar and vanilla. Beat in one egg at a time with mixer. Sift all dry ingredients together. Add to first mixture, mix well. Add pineapple, carrots and nuts. Bake in greased and floured oblong pan, 9 x 12 x 2 at 350° for about 50 - 60 minutes.

FROSTING:

1 - 3 oz. pkg. cream cheese	1 T margarine
1 1/2 cups powdered sugar	1 tsp. vanilla

Melt margarine and add cream cheese. Add other ingredients, beat well.

A good moist cake.

PEANUT BUTTER CAKE

1/2 cup shortening	2 cups cake flour, sifted
1/2 cup peanut butter	2 1/2 tsp. baking powder
1 1/2 cups brown sugar, packed	1/2 tsp. salt
2 eggs, beaten	1 tsp. vanilla
2/3 cup milk	

Cream shortening, peanut butter and sugar. Beat in eggs in 2 parts, add vanilla. Sift dry ingredients together, add alternately with milk. Bake in oblong pan, greased and floured, at 325° - 350° for about 40 - 45 minutes.

TOPPING:

1/4 cup peanut butter	1/4 cup margarine
1/4 cup brown sugar	2 T water
3/4 cup nuts	

Mix all together. Spread on cake when cake is done. Return cake to oven for 10 minutes.

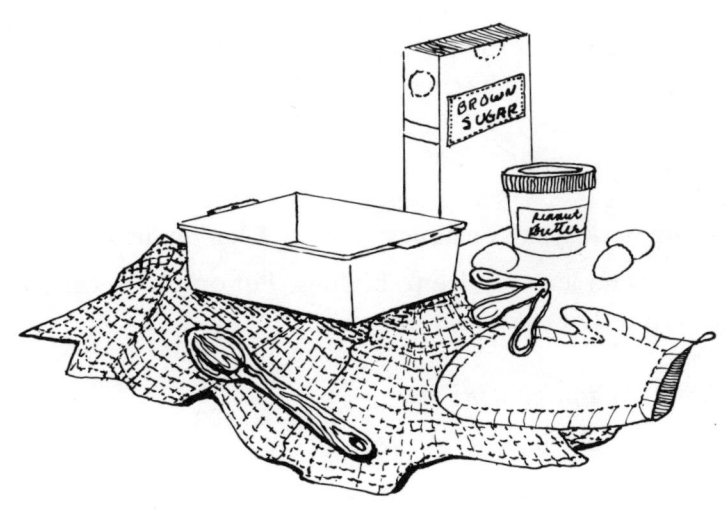

DARK FRUIT CAKE

1 cup margarine	2 3/4 cups flour (*browned)
1 cup brown sugar (packed)	1 tsp. soda
1/4 cup dark corn syrup	2 tsp. baking powder
1/4 cup molasses	1/2 tsp. salt
5 eggs, beaten	1/2 tsp. cinnamon
grated rind of 1 lemon & 1 orange	1/2 tsp. nutmeg
	1/4 tsp. cloves
1 lb. raisins cooked in 1/2 cup water, chopped	1/4 cup orange juice
	1 1/2 cups mixed fruits (candied)
1 lb. dates, cut up	
1 1/2 cups nuts, chopped	1 cup candied cherries, cut up

*To brown flour, put in heavy skillet on burner, low heat, stirring most of the time till it turns a tan color.

Cream margarine with sugar, syrup and molasses. Add beaten eggs, half at a time, beat well. Sift dry ingredients together. Sift 1/4 cup flour over nuts and fruits and stir gently. Add dry ingredients with orange juice. Add fruits and nuts last. Bake in round tube cake pan. It makes one large cake or two medium ones. (Large cake — 4 to 5 lbs.) Grease and flour pan. Line pan with brown paper, then wax paper. Bake slowly 250° - 275° for 2 to 2 1/2 hours. Keep pan of water in bottom of oven while baking.

GLAZE FOR CAKE:

1/4 cup dark syrup or honey   2 T lemon juice

Heat syrup and lemon juice to boiling. Put on top of cake while it is still warm. Let cake cool in pan.

This has been a prize winner.

ICINGS

ICINGS

SEVEN MINUTE ICING

5 T water	pinch of salt
1/4 tsp. cream of tartar	1 1/2 cups sugar
2 large egg whites	1 tsp. plain gelatin
2 T water	1/4 tsp. vanilla

In double boiler, put water, salt, cream of tartar, sugar and egg whites. Dissolve gelatin in 2 T water and set aside. Cook first mixture in double boiler, beating with electric mixer till it will stand in peaks. Turn off heat. Add gelatin and beat well. Add vanilla. Beat till thick and creamy. Spread icing on cool cake.

✦I✦

CHOCOLATE ICING

3 cups granulated sugar	1/2 tsp. salt
1/4 cup margarine	2 oz. baking chocolate, melted
pinch of soda	
	1 1/4 cups whole milk and cream or ½ & ½

Heat milk. Add sugar, stirring constantly. Add soda to keep from curdling. Boil fast, add margarine. Cook to soft ball stage, or 230° with a thermometer. Add chocolate when done. Cool a few minutes and beat till creamy.

✦I✦

BUTTER ICING

2 1/2 T warm milk	1/4 cup margarine
2 cups powdered sugar	1/2 tsp. vanilla

Add margarine to warm milk. Beat in powdered sugar and vanilla. Beat all till smooth and creamy. If too thin, add more powdered sugar. Cover tightly till ready to use.

CARAMEL ICING

1 cup firmly packed brown sugar	2 cups granulated sugar
	1/4 tsp. salt
1 1/4 cups whole milk or part cream	1/2 tsp. vanilla
	pinch of soda
1/4 cup margarine	

Heat liquid, add sugars, stirring all the time. Add soda to keep from curdling. Add margarine, boil quickly to soft ball stage or with thermometer, to 232°. Cool for a few minutes, beat till creamy.

•ı•

BUTTER CREAM FROSTING

1/4 cup margarine	1/2 lb. powdered sugar
1 egg, or 1 egg yolk	1 T milk
1/4 tsp. vanilla	1/4 tsp. salt

Beat egg, add milk. Add part of sugar. Beat in margarine, vanilla, and rest of sugar. Beat till creamy. Cover tightly till ready to use.

•ı•

ORANGE GLAZE

3 T margarine at room temperature	1 egg yolk
	1 tsp. lemon juice
1/2 tsp. grated orange rind	1 1/2 T orange juice
2 cups powdered sugar	

Beat all ingredients together, except the powdered sugar and orange juice, then beat them in. Good to keep on hand in the refrigerator to ice cake or cookies.

PIES and COBBLERS

PIES and COBBLERS

PEACH COBBLER

FILLING:

Prepare 4 cups fresh peaches or 1 large, drained can of peaches. Mix 1/4 cup peach juice, 1/2 cup sugar (use 3/4 cup sugar with fresh peaches) and 1 1/2 tsp. tapioca, 1 T lemon juice, 1 T margarine. Let stand while preparing pie crust. Use 8 x 8 x 2 pan.

CRUST:

3 cups flour	1 cup shortening
1 T salt	1 egg, well beaten
6 T cold water	1 tsp. vinegar

Cut salt and shortening into flour with blender or fork or use two table knives. Add the egg–water–vinegar mixture, 2 T at a time. Handle *lightly*. Roll out on floured pastry cloth, a portion large enough to fit pan. Place in pan. Add peaches, wet edge of dough. Roll another piece of dough large enough to cover top of pan, cut holes in top, press edges of dough together, flute edges. Bake at 450° for 15 minutes, then reduce heat to 375°. Bake till juice bubbles up through holes in top crust. Cool, serve warm or cold with whipped topping, whipped cream or ice cream.

I have won on this in 1974 and 1975. It was judged the best of the peach cookery and I won a Purple Rosette and a Trophy.

[handwritten:]
Pie crust
1 1/3 flour
1 1/2 tsp. salt
1/2 c lard scant
3 T. water

APPLE PIE WITH COCONUT CRUMB TOP

    1/2 cup sugar   1/4 tsp. cinnamon
1 1/2 T minute tapioca   3/8 tsp. salt
    1/4 tsp. nutmeg   1 T lemon juice
      5 cups peeled and thinly sliced apples
        Never Fail Pie Crust

Combine sugar, salt, spices, and tapioca with apples and lemon juice. Line 8 inch pan with Never Fail Pie Crust, pour apple mixture in. Bake at 425° for 15 minutes. Reduce heat to 350° for 25 minutes. Remove from oven to put on topping.

CRUMB TOPPING:

    1/2 cup graham cracker crumbs
    1/3 cup brown sugar
    1/4 cup soft margarine   } COMBINE
    1/2 cup flaked coconut

Have topping ready, spread over apples, add coconut last. Return to oven for 15 minutes longer. A piece of foil may be laid over top of apples at the beginning to steam and cook apples.

◆I◆

LEMON PIE

1 cup sugar   5 T cornstarch
2 cups water   1/8 tsp. salt
3 T lemon juice   2 T margarine
3 egg yolks, beaten with a little water

Mix sugar, cornstarch, salt, and water. Cook. Add egg yolks, lemon juice, and margarine just before it is cooked completely. Have a baked pie crust (8 or 9 inch) ready. Be sure the filling is cold before pouring into crust. Cover with meringue and bake until lightly browned at 350°.

APPLE COBBLER

Use either canned or fresh apples. Use a pan about 8 x 8 x 2 inches. I use the Never Fail Pie Crust recipe on page 66 in this book. Line pan with rolled out dough. If using raw apples, peel and slice, and use about 6 apples.

1 cup sugar	1 T quick tapioca
1/2 cup water	1/8 tsp. cinnamon
1 T lemon juice	1/8 tsp. nutmeg
1 tsp. butter or margarine	

Mix all ingredients with apples and pour into pan. Roll out more dough, moisten edge of dough in pan, place top dough over apples, seal edges, cut off surplus dough. Slash top of dough to let steam out. Bake at 450° till top starts to brown. Reduce heat to 375°. Bake till apples are cooked, about 1 hour. Cut in squares, serve warm with whipped topping.

Very good.

◆I◆

RAISIN CREAM PIE

1 cup raisins	1/3 cup sugar
1/3 cup syrup	3 T cornstarch
2 egg yolks	1 1/4 cups milk
1/2 tsp. vanilla	pinch of salt

Cook raisins in water. Drain and cool. Mix cornstarch in sugar. Beat egg yolks with a little milk. Add all other ingredients. Cook over low heat till thick. Cool. Pour in baked pie shell. Beat 2 egg whites till fairly stiff. Beat in 4 T sugar. Spread on pie filling. Bake in 350° oven till lightly browned.

RHUBARB PIE WITH MERINGUE

    2 cups fresh rhubarb (cut in 1 inch pieces)
1/2 cup water
    1 T flour   1 cup sugar
    2 egg yolks, beaten   2 T butter

Cook rhubarb and water to heat through. Add other ingredients and cook till thick. Cool. Add to baked pie shell, medium size.

MERINGUE:

    2 egg whites   4 T sugar

Beat egg whites until stiff. Add sugar. Beat till mixture stands in firm peaks. Spread on pie filling. Bake in oven at 350° till lightly browned.

My mother made this one many times.

CHOCOLATE CHIP PIE

3 T cornstarch	1/8 tsp. salt
1/2 cup sugar	2 egg yolks
2 cups milk	1/2 tsp. vanilla
1/2 cup chocolate chips	

Mix sugar with cornstarch and salt. Beat egg yolks with a little milk. Add rest of milk and first mixture. Cook in heavy pan, stirring constantly till thick. Remove from burner. Stir in vanilla and chocolate chips. Stir until chips are all dissolved. When cold, pour in baked pie crust.

MERINGUE:

1/8 tsp. cream of tartar	2 egg whites
4 T sugar	1/4 tsp. vanilla

Beat egg whites to soft peaks. Add cream of tartar. Add sugar, 2 T at a time. Add vanilla. Beat to stiff peaks. Spread over pie. Brown lightly in 350° oven.

A new one, but good.

•I•

PUMPKIN PIE

Prepare 9 inch unbaked pastry shell, using Never Fail Pie Crust.

2 eggs, beaten	1/4 tsp. cinnamon
1 cup sugar	1/4 tsp. ginger
1 1/2 cups pumpkin	1/8 tsp. cloves
1/2 tsp. salt	1 3/4 cups milk or part cream

Blend salt and spices with sugar. Stir pumpkin into eggs. Add sugar. Gradually add milk, stirring till well mixed. Pour filling into pastry shell. Bake in hot oven, 450° for 10 - 15 minutes. Reduce heat to 375° for about 30 minutes or till it puffs up in middle of filling.

CHIFFON PUMPKIN PIE

1 T unflavored gelatin	1/4 cup cold water
3 egg yolks	1/2 cup sugar
1/4 tsp. salt	1 cup cooked pumpkin
1/3 cup milk	1/4 tsp. cinnamon
a dash of cloves	3 egg whites
1/3 cup sugar	

Soften gealtin in cold water. Beat egg yolks till thick. Add salt, pumpkin, 1/2 cup sugar, spices, and milk. Cook mixture on low heat about 5 minutes, until thick. Add gelatin and stir until it is dissolved. Beat egg whites until stiff and add 1/3 cup sugar. Beat in sugar till quite stiff. Fold into pumpkin mixture. Pour in baked pie crust and chill. Serve with whipped topping.

A tried and true recipe.

MINCEMEAT (My Mother's)

2 lb. cooked lean beef, cut fine	1/2 gal. peeled, quartered apples, cooked briefly with 1 cup water
1 cup suet, cut up	
1 lb. seeded raisins	1/2 gal. sweet apple cider
1 T salt	2 cups sugar, (or more)
1 tsp. cinnamon	1/2 tsp. nutmeg
1 lb. seedless raisins	

Put all together in large pan. Cook slowly for 1 hour. Add spices near end of cooking. Can while hot in sterilized jars using sterilized lids and seal while hot.

PEACH CRUMBLE

1 can (No 2½ size) drained peaches
2 tsp. lemon juice
1 tsp. grated lemon rind
1/3 cup sugar
1/4 cup peach juice

Arrange sliced peaches in greased baking dish. Mix the above ingredients and pour over peaches.

TOPPING:

6 T flour
1/4 tsp. cinnamon
6 T sugar
3 T margarine

Cut margarine into dry ingredients with a knife until crumbly and spread over top of peaches. Bake at 375° for 30 - 35 minutes. Serve hot or cold with whipped topping or whipped cream.

NEVER FAIL PIE CRUST

3 cups flour	1 tsp. salt
1 cup lard or shortening	1 egg
6 T cold water	1 tsp. vinegar

Cut shortening in flour and salt with blender or fork. Beat egg, add water and vinegar. Add to dry mixture 2 T at a time. Handle dough lightly. Roll dough on floured pastry cloth. Fit into pan and cut off extra over edge of pan. Flute the edge of the dough and prick with fork to keep it from blistering. Bake at 450° till lightly browned 10 - 15 minutes. Makes top and bottom crust or bottom crusts for two pies. Use with any kind of pie.

Good to the last crumb.

◆I◆

MERINGUE FOR CREAM PIES

Beat 3 egg whites with 1/4 tsp. cream of tartar and a dash of salt to soft peaks.

Add 6 T sugar, 2 T at a time. Beat to a firm peak or till sugar is all melted. Test between fingers till you can not feel any grains. Do not put pie filling in baked crust until filling is cold. Then spread meringue on top. Put in a 350° oven to brown lightly, 10 - 15 min.

You will not have syrup beads form on top if you follow this recipe.

HONEY RECIPES

HONEY RECIPES

If you like honey, you will like these honey recipes. I have won on all of them at the Illinois State Fair.

HONEY SPICE CAKE

1/2 cup shortening	3/4 cup honey
3/4 cup sugar	3 eggs
1 cup milk, or water	1/2 tsp. salt
3 cups cake flour, sifted	2 1/2 tsp. baking powder
1 tsp. cinnamon	1/2 tsp. cloves
1/4 tsp. nutmeg	1/4 tsp. allspice

Cream shortening and honey well, then cream in sugar, using mixer. Sift all dry ingredients together. Beat in eggs one at a time before adding flour and liquid. Beat till smooth. Bake in two 8 x 8 x 2 greased and floured pans with waxed paper in bottoms, in a 325° oven for 45 minutes. Cool for 15 minutes in pans.

ICING:

1 1/2 cups sugar	4 T water
2 egg whites	1/4 tsp. cream of tartar
1 tsp. plain gelatin	

Combine sugar, egg whites, 3 T water and cream of tartar. Cook in double boiler, beating all the time for about 5 minutes. Add gelatin dissolved with 1 T water. Add it at end of cooking and beat in. Beat till ready to spread.

HONEY DEVIL'S FOOD CAKE

- 3/4 cup shortening
- 1 cup honey   } CREAM TOGETHER
- 1 cup sugar

3 eggs	1 cup water
1/2 tsp. salt	1 tsp. baking powder
1 tsp. soda	3 cups flour

3 oz. melted baking chocolate (unsweetened)

Add eggs to creamed mixture, one egg at a time, and beat in. Add melted chocolate. Add dry ingredients and water alternately. Bake in two large cake pans 9 x 9 x 2, greased and floured, with wax paper lining in bottom, at 325° for about 1 hour.

HONEY ICING:

3 cups sugar	1/4 cup honey
2 oz. chocolate, melted	1 cup coffee cream or ½ & ½

Mix ingredients. Cook over low burner till about ready to boil, then boil, stirring constantly, until it reaches the soft ball stage. Cool and beat till creamy. If too thick, add a little cream.

This is such a good cake.

WHITE HONEY CAKE

2/3 cup shortening	1/4 cup margarine
1 cup honey	3/4 tsp. salt
1 2/3 cups water	6 egg whites
4 1/2 cups cake flour, sifted	4 tsp. baking powder

Beat shortening and honey well. (Keep honey in refrigerator). Add flour and salt alternately with water. Beat egg whites quite stiff. Sift baking powder over beaten egg whites and add last, fold in *lightly* by hand. Bake in two 8 x 8 x 2 inch pans. Grease and flour bottom of pans, also line with waxed paper. Bake at 300° for one hour. Ice with Seven Minute Icing. Add a little honey to flavor it. Sprinkle coconut on icing.

Yes, a Blue Ribbon winner.

◆I◆

HONEY FRUIT BARS

1/4 cup margarine	2/3 cup flour, sifted
1/3 cup honey	1/2 tsp. baking powder
2 eggs, beaten	1/2 tsp. salt
1/2 cup nuts	1 cup dates, cut up
1/4 cup raisins	1/2 cup candied cherries, cut up

Cream margarine and honey, add eggs. Add dry ingredients. Last stir in nuts and fruits. Bake in 8 x 8 x 2 greased pan at 300° for about 40 - 50 minutes. When cool, cut into bars.

I entered these in 1975, at the Illinois State Fair and won a Blue Ribbon. It was also judged the best of honey cookery.

HONEY GINGER BREAD

1/2 cup margarine
1 egg, beaten
1 1/2 tsp. soda
1 tsp. cinnamon
1/2 tsp. salt

1 1/2 cups honey
2 1/2 cups flour
1 tsp. ginger
1/2 tsp. cloves
1 cup hot water

Cream margarine and honey. Add beaten egg. Sift flour, soda, ginger, cinnamon, cloves and salt. Mix all together. Last, add hot water. Mix well. Bake in oblong pan at 325° about 30 minutes.

HONEY DATE NUT BREAD

2 T shortening
1 egg, beaten
1/4 tsp. soda
1 cup whole wheat flour
1 cup dates, cut up

3/4 cup honey
1/4 tsp. salt
1 cup white flour
3/4 cup nuts
1 cup water

Cook the dates and 1 cup water until thick. Set aside to cool. Cream shortening and honey. Add beaten egg. Add flour and other dry ingredients with date mixture and nuts. Bake in greased and floured bread pan at 325° for 1 hour. Cool on rack.

Good and chewy.

CARROT HONEY COOKIES

1 cup flour	1/4 tsp. cinnamon
1/4 tsp. nutmeg	1/8 tsp. salt
1/4 cup butter	1 tsp. soda
1/2 cup honey	1 egg, beaten
1/2 cup raisins	1/2 cup grated, raw carrots
1/4 cup nuts, chopped	1/2 cup quick, dry oats

Cream together butter and honey. Add beaten egg, salt and soda. Sift flour and spices. Add to other ingredients. Add oats, raisins, carrots and nuts. Chill dough, then drop by teaspoons on teflon cookie sheet. Bake at 325° - 350° for 10 - 12 minutes.

A Blue Ribbon winner.

•I•

HONEY HERMITS

1/2 cup shortening	1 small egg, beaten
2/3 cup honey	1 cup white flour
1/2 tsp. salt	1/2 cup whole wheat flour
1/2 tsp. soda	1/4 tsp. cinnamon
1/4 tsp. nutmeg	1/4 cup nuts, chopped
1 cup dates, cut up	1 cup raisins, cut up

Cream shortening and honey. Sift together, flours, cinnamon, and nutmeg. Add beaten egg to creamed mixture. Add dry ingredients. Add nuts and fruits last. Drop by teaspoon on greased cookie sheet. Bake at 350° for 10 - 12 minutes or less if they get too brown. They stay very moist in closed container.

A Fair winner.

HONEY OATMEAL COOKIES

1/4 cup butter	1/2 cup honey
1 egg, beaten	1/2 cup raisins
1/3 cup water	3/4 cup flour
1/8 tsp. salt	1/2 tsp. soda
1/4 tsp. nutmeg	1/4 tsp. cinnamon
3/4 cup quick, dry oats	

Boil raisins in 1/3 cup water for 5 minutes. Cool and set aside. Sift together flour, salt, soda, nutmeg and cinnamon. Cream butter and honey together, add egg. Add dry ingredients with raisins and liquid. Add 3/4 cup quick, dry oats. Chill dough 1 hour. Drop by spoonfuls on teflon pan. Bake at 350° for 10 - 12 minutes.

A good moist cookie and a winner.

◆|◆

SPICY PINEAPPLE HONEY GLAZE FOR HAM

1 - 13 1/2 oz. can crushed pineapple	
1 - 12 oz. can apricot pineapple nectar	
1/4 cup tomato catsup	1 tsp. dry mustard
1 T Worcestershire sauce	1/2 cup honey

Combine all, heat to simmering. Good to bake on ham.

HONEY WHITE BREAD

3 cups sifted flour	1/2 cup scalded milk
1 T shortening	1 tsp. salt
3 T honey	1/2 cup warm water
1/2 package dry yeast	

Add shortening to hot milk and cool. Add yeast to 1/2 cup warm water. Mix all ingredients together and knead on floured board for 5 minutes. Put in greased bowl and let rise in warm place till double in bulk for a finer grain bread. Push down and turn dough over and let rise the second time. Make into one loaf, pan size 8 x 4 x 3, and let rise till light. Bake at 350° for 45 minutes.

•I•

HONEY RYE BREAD

3/4 cup warm water	1 pkg. dry yeast
1 cup scalded milk, cooled	2 tsp. salt
1/4 cup honey	2 T shortening
2 cups white flour	4 cups rye flour

Dissolve yeast in water. Combine all ingredients. Knead on floured bread board for 5 minutes. Put in large greased bowl, let rise until double in bulk, punch down, let rise again. Mold in two loaves and let rise in pans 8 x 4 x 3 till light. Bake at 375° for 45 minutes.

HONEY RAISIN BREAD

1 cup scalded milk, cooled	1 tsp. sugar
1/2 pkg. yeast	3 1/2 cups sifted flour
1/4 cup margarine	1/4 cup honey
1 tsp. salt	1 egg, beaten
1/2 cup raisins	

Add sugar and yeast to cooled milk. To yeast mixture, add half of flour. Beat and let rise one hour. Add softened margarine, honey, beaten egg, salt and raisins. Beat well and add rest of flour. (Reserve some flour to use in kneading.) Knead for 5' minutes. Put in greased bowl and turn dough over to grease top. Let rise till double in bulk. Punch down and let rest 15 minutes. Knead air bubbles out. Roll out, then roll up as a jelly roll and seal edges. Put in pan 8 x 4 x 3. Let rise till double in bulk. Bake at 350º for about 45 minutes.

A State Fair winner for several years.

♦I♦

HONEY WHOLE WHEAT BREAD

1 cup scalded milk, cooled	2 T honey
1 tsp. salt	1 T shortening
1/2 cake or 1/2 pkg. yeast	2 cups whole wheat flour
1 1/2 cups white flour	

Dissolve yeast in liquid. Put flours in large bowl and stir in all the above ingredients, then work and knead on floured board for 5 minutes. Place in greased bowl and cover in warm place till it rises double in bulk. Punch down, turn over and let rise again. Mold into loaf and place in pan 9 x 4 x 3. Let rise to top of pan. Bake at 350º for 40 - 45 minutes.

A good winner at the State Fair.

DESSERTS and SALADS

DESSERTS AND SALADS

DESSERT CHERRY SALAD

Crust:

1 1/2 cups graham cracker crumbs   1 stick margarine, softened

Mix crumbs and margarine together. Put a layer in bottom of oblong baking dish. Save some for the top. Chill in refrigerator.

Filling:

2 cups whipped topping   3 oz. pkg. cream cheese

Beat together and spread on top of crumbs.

Topping:

1 can of cherry pie filling (size No. 303)

Spread cherry pie filling on cheese mixture. Put rest of cracker crumbs over top. Chill for several hours or overnight in refrigerator.

Good eating!

•I•

MARSHMALLOW SALAD

1/2 pint whipping cream   2-3 oz. pkgs. cream cheese
1/2 cup salad dressing   1 large can drained fruit cocktail
1-4 oz. bottle maraschino cherries, drained

Whip the cream and crumble the cheese into whipped cream. Fold in salad dressing, fruit cocktail and drained cherries. Chill a few hours before serving.

GOLDEN APRICOT SALAD

Dissolve 1 package orange flavored gelatin in 1 cup boiling water or fruit juice. Add 1/4 tsp. dry mustard, 1/4 tsp. salt, 2 tsp. lemon juice, chill. When slightly thickened, fold in 1/4 cup mayonnaise, 2 cups dried apricots (cooked), 3/4 cup diced celery, 1/4 cup pecan meats (broken), 1/4 cup sugar. Chill until firm. Unmold on lettuce leaves. Garnish with mayonnaise. Serves 8.

•❖•

JELLO SALAD

1 - 3 oz. box lime jello　　　1 - 8 oz. pkg. cream cheese
1 - 8 oz. pkg. bite size marshmallows

Pour 1 cup boiling water over the above ingredients. Stir, let cool. Add:

1 cup whipped topping　　　1/2 cup salad dressing

Whip mixture.
Add:

1 cup crushed pineapple　　　1 cup nuts

When set, top with a layer of orange or lemon jello prepared according to directions on the package.

Very good.

PUDDING JELLO

Mix:
- 1 - 3 oz. pkg. orange jello
- 1 - 3 oz. pkg. tapioca pudding
- 1 - 3 oz. pkg. vanilla pudding (not instant)
- 3 cups water

Cook until clear and add:
- 1 cup pineapple juice
- 1 cup mandarin oranges, drained
- 1 - 13 oz. can crushed pineapple, drained

Chill overnight, or use only 1/2 cup fruit juice if you wish to serve sooner. Serve with whipped topping.

Try this one.

•I•

GRAHAM CRACKER CHEESE CAKE

Crust:
- 1/4 lb. margarine
- 34 graham crackers (rolled fine)
- 2 T powdered sugar

Filling:
- 1 cup hot water
- 1 can whipped, evaporated milk
- 1 pkg. lemon jello
- 1/2 cup sugar
- 1/2 lb. cream cheese

Blend margarine, powdered sugar and graham crackers. Press mixture in bottom and sides of 9-1/2 x 13 greased pan, keeping back 1 cup for the top. Chill crust in refrigerator. Combine jello, hot water, and sugar. When cool, add whipped milk and cream cheese. Beat together and pour into crumb crust. Add remaining crumbs on top. Chill in refrigerator for at least 12 hours.

Good for dessert anytime.

CREAM PUFFS

1 cup sifted flour	1 cup hot water
4 eggs	1/2 cup butter

Add butter to hot water in large saucepan and place over direct heat. When butter melts, add flour all at once. Stir constantly. Cook until mixture leaves sides of pan in a smooth, compact ball. Remove from heat, add eggs one at a time, beating vigorously after each addition till smooth. Drop by tablespoon, 2 inches apart, on greased cookie sheet. Bake at 425° for 15 minutes, reduce heat to 350° for 20 minutes longer. When you serve them, fill with a filling of your choice.

Good any time, for a club dessert, or at home. Also a Fair winner.

CANDIES

CANDIES

PEANUT BRITTLE

2 cups sugar	1 tsp. butter
1 cup light corn syrup	1/2 tsp, vanilla
2 cups shelled, raw peanuts	2 tsp. soda
1/2 cup water	1 tsp. salt

Cook sugar, syrup, and water until very thick ($270°$ on thermometer), then add butter, salt and peanuts. Stir well and cook until nuts start to brown (the skins will pop open). Remove from heat at once. Stir in vanilla, and all the soda at once. Stir till it foams up. Pour on greased slab, or back of heavy greased cookie sheets. Tip pan and pour out as a pancake. Never spread with a knife. As soon as cool enough to handle, loosen with a knife, turn over and stretch from edges by pulling to make as thin as possible. When cold break in pieces. Keep in closed container.

I have made this many times and won first at the Illinois State Fair.

•|•

CHOCOLATE FUDGE

2 cups sugar	1/3 cup white corn syrup
1/2 cup rich milk (or ½ &½)	2 T butter
1 1/2 squares chocolate	1 tsp. vanilla
pinch of salt	

Mix sugar, milk, chocolate, salt and syrup. Cook over slow fire until it will form a soft ball in cold water. Remove from fire and let stand by setting pan in cold water until cool, adding butter and vanilla last. Beat until creamy and pour on buttered platter. Nuts can be added while beating. Cut in squares when firm.

AUNT BILL'S BROWN CANDY

- 2 cups granulated sugar, melted in heavy pan (not burned) use low fire
- 4 cups granulated sugar ⎫ Bring to boil while melting
- 2 cups ½ and ½ ⎭ first sugar.

Pour thin stream of melted sugar into boiling sugar and cream mixture, stirring rapidly. Boil and stir to a firm ball stage in cold water (238 - 239°). Turn off heat, add 1/4 tsp. soda and stir in as it foams up. Add 1/4 cup butter, stir as it melts. Set aside for 20 minutes to cool. Beat till it loses glossy sheen. Quickly add 2 lb. pecans, spread into buttered pans. Makes 6 lbs.

Very Delicious

•❖•

DIVINITY CANDY

- 2 1/2 cups white sugar
- 1/2 cup white corn syrup
- 1/2 cup water
- 1/2 tsp. vanilla
- 1/8 tsp. salt
- 2 egg whites
- 1/4 tsp. cream of tartar

Beat egg whites with salt and cream of tartar till stiff. Cook sugar, syrup and water till soft ball stage forms in cold water. Pour half of hot syrup over beaten egg whites, beating constantly. Add 1/2 tsp. vanilla. Cook rest of syrup until it forms a hard ball and beat into egg whites. Drop by teaspoons on greased platter.

•❖•

POPCORN CRISPS

- 2 cups sugar
- 1/2 cup water
- 1 1/2 cups dark corn syrup
- 1 T butter

Cook sugar, syrup and water to hard ball stage, then add butter. Stir till light brown (takes only a few moments, be careful not to burn it).

Pour it over six quarts of popped corn, sprinkle with salt while stirring. Spread on cookie sheets to cool.

CASSEROLES and SOUP

CASSEROLES and SOUP

CHICKEN VEGETABLE CASSEROLE

1 frying chicken, cut up
Seasoned flour for coating chicken
1/4 cup shortening
3/4 cup milk
1 303 can small peas, drained
1 303 can small potatoes, drained
2 10 oz. cans cream of chicken soup

Coat chicken pieces with flour. Heat shortening in frying pan. Brown chicken on both sides. Arrange pieces in shallow casserole dish. Add peas and potatoes. Mix milk with soup and pour over vegetables. Bake uncovered at 350° for 40 to 50 minutes, or until chicken is tender.

✦l✦

SCALLOPED CORN

1 can cream style corn
1 can whole kernel corn, drained
16 crushed soda crackers
1 1/2 cups milk
2 eggs, beaten
1 tsp. salt
2 T sugar
1/4 cup margarine, melted

Mix all together and pour in buttered casserole dish. Bake at 325° - 350° for about 1 hour.

Quick and easy to prepare.

TURKEY LOAF

*1 lb. ground uncooked turkey	1/2 cup milk
1 tsp. ground sage	1/4 cup chopped onion
1/4 cup catsup	2 slices white bread
2 tsp. salt	1/8 tsp. pepper
1/4 cup chopped celery	1/2 cup tomato juice

Soak bread in milk, add all other ingredients, except tomato juice. Mold in a loaf. Place in a glass baking dish, pour tomato juice over loaf. Bake 1 hour at 350°.

*Frozen, ground, uncooked turkey may be found in the frozen food section of your grocery store.

•|•

SWEET POTATO CASSEROLE

2 cans sweet potatoes (each 17 oz.)	2 large apples (peeled, cored and sliced)
1 tsp. salt	1 tsp. grated lemon rind
1/8 tsp. cinnamon	1/4 cup butter
1/3 cup white syrup	

Mix together syrup, butter, lemon rind, salt and cinnamon. In a two quart baking dish, alternate layers of sweet potatoes and apples, beginning with sweet potatoes and ending with apples to make 4 layers. Evenly drizzle about 1/4 cup of syrup mixture over each layer. Bake in pre-heated oven at 350° basting occasionally until apples are cooked through, about one hour. Makes 8 servings.

CHICKEN DIVAN

   1 pkg. (10 oz.) frozen asparagus or broccoli spears
   3 or 4 servings sliced cooked chicken or turkey
   1 can cream of chicken soup
1/3 cup milk
1/3 cup shredded cheddar cheese

Arrange asparagus in 1 1/2 qt. shallow baking dish, 10 x 6 x 2, top with chicken. Combine soup with cheese and milk. Pour over chicken. Bake at 450° for 15 minutes or until hot. Makes 3 or 4 servings.

◆I◆

SALMON PATTIES

  1 large can salmon (flaked apart)
  1 T mustard   1/4 tsp. pepper
1/2 cup milk   2 eggs, beaten
     Soda cracker crumbs   1 T flour

Mix salmon, pepper and mustard together. Mix eggs, milk and flour in heavy pan and cook slowly, stirring constantly, until quite thick. Add salmon mixture and cracker crumbs (about 4 crackers). Let cool. Make into patties, roll in cracker crumbs. Heat corn oil in skillet. Fry patties brown on each side. Serve with lemon wedges.

SCALLOPED CHICKEN

1 pint cooked, cut up chicken	1 pint chicken broth
1 cup whole milk	1 T flour
2 T butter	a few shakes of pepper
1/2 tsp. salt	1/2 tsp. sage
1/2 cup celery, cut up	6 crushed soda crackers
crushed bread crumbs	

Mix chicken, broth, milk, flour and butter together. Place pepper, salt, sage, celery and cracker crumbs in bottom of greased baking dish. Add all other ingredients. Add crushed bread crumbs on top. Bake at 375° till lightly browned.

•I•

MACARONI AND CHEESE

1-7 oz. pkg. macaroni, (cooked)	1/2 lb. cheese
	1 1/2 cups milk
2 T margarine	2 T flour

In a sauce pan, melt margarine and blend in flour. Add milk all at once, cook till thick. Reduce heat and add cheese. Cook till cheese is melted. Combine this with macaroni in baking dish. Cover and bake at 350° about 30 minutes. Take lid off last 10 minutes to brown the top.

ONIONS BAKED IN TOMATO JUICE

8 medium sized onions
1 cup tomato juice
1/8 tsp. pepper
2 T butter
1 tsp. salt
3 T corn syrup

Peel onions. Place in greased casserole. Combine melted butter, tomato juice, seasonings and syrup. Pour around onions, cover and bake in 350° oven until onions are tender, about 1 hour.

Very good.

SALMON EGG CASSEROLE

1 large can salmon (flaked apart)
6 hard boiled eggs
1 medium onion, chopped
1/4 cup flour
1/8 tsp. pepper
1 cup cooked rice
1/4 cup margarine
1 cup chopped celery
1 tsp. salt
1 1/2 cups milk

Melt margarine in sauce pan. Add onion and celery. Saute 10 minutes on low heat. Stir in flour, salt and pepper. Gradually stir in milk. Cook slowly until mixture is thick. Arrange rice in bottom of greased casserole. Top with salmon, slice eggs over salmon. Pour sauce over all and bake in pre-heated oven 350° for 25 - 30 minutes. Serve with sour cream if desired.

NOODLES

    1 egg, beaten   1/4 tsp. salt
    4 T cream or canned milk   1 cup flour
    1/2 tsp. baking powder

Mix all together. Roll out about 1/4 inch thick and cut in strips. Drop in boiling hot broth and simmer for 15 - 20 minutes. Drain and serve.

•I•

VEGETABLE SOUP

Step I — Soup Stock

Put beef bones and bony pieces of chicken in a large kettle. Cover with water. Skim several times. Simmer for about 3 hrs. Remove bones, add cut up lean meat if desired.

Step II — Vegetables

Peel and cut in pieces -carrots, potatoes, onions, tomatoes (use canned if fresh not available) and celery. Add about 1/2 cup uncooked rice, if desired. Cook all together in water just to cover, till tender. Add broth. Cook slowly for 2 or 3 hours. Season to taste with salt and pepper.

PRESERVES
JAMS
JELLIES
and BUTTERS

PRESERVES, JAMS, JELLIES, AND BUTTERS

APRICOT PRESERVES

Peel, seed, and cut in halves, enough apricots to make 1 1/2 lbs. Make a syrup of 1 cup water, 1 1/2 lbs. sugar. Boil till it threads, then add fruit. Boil about 10 minutes. Skim off foam. Add 2 T lemon juice and boil 2 minutes longer. Shake in pan while cooling, then can in sterilized jars using sterilized lids.

First prize winner in 1974 and 1975. A trophy in 1974.

PEACH PRESERVES

Peel and seed yellow peaches. To 1 3/4 lb. fruit, make a syrup of 1 cup water to 1 1/2 cups sugar. Add fruit and cook slowly for 10 minutes. Add 2 T lemon juice and boil 5 minutes more. Cook with asbestos pad under pan to keep from sticking or with a very low fire. Cool in pan till thick. Can in sterilized jars using sterilized lids.

Another prize winner.

CHERRY PRESERVES

Seed 1 quart of ripe cherries. For each pound of cherries make a syrup of 3/4 lb. sugar to 1 cup water in sauce pan. Boil water and half of sugar about 5 minutes. Add washed cherries and boil slowly. Then add rest of sugar and boil about 10 minutes more. Add 1 T of lemon juice and boil about 5 minutes longer. Skim off foam. Cool in pan and shake pan to fluff up cherries. Can in sterilized jars using sterilized lids and seal. Add paraffin wax to help keep a better seal.

Always a good Blue Ribbon winner. Just won on them in 1975, as the best overall preserves, jams and jellies. I also won a trophy.

•I•

STRAWBERRY PRESERVES

Stem and wash enough ripe large berries to make the following:

- **4 cups strawberries (rounded)**
- **5 cups sugar**

Use large flat pan. Wet bottom of pan with 1/4 cup water. Put layer of sugar then layer of berries, more sugar, then berries. Do not double recipe. Cover with lid, let stand for 2 hours. Then put on low heat, till juice forms. Boil for 8 minutes, stirring at times and skimming off foam. Add 4 T of lemon juice and boil 2 more minutes. Cool in pan and while they cool, shake the pan around to fluff up berries. Can when cold and seal with hot sterilized lids.

This one is always a Blue Ribbon winner -- first in 1974 and 1975.

STRAWBERRY JAM

Crush ripe, firm strawberries. To 4 cups crushed berries, add 2 cups sugar. Heat on stove, stirring and boil 5 minutes. Then add 2 more cups sugar and 2 T lemon juice and boil for about ten minutes. Skim off foam. Cool briefly, then can in sterilized jars using sterilized lids.

Good.

•|•

BASIC JAM RECIPE

    4 cups prepared fruit (berries, diced or crushed apricots, peaches, plums, etc.)
    4 cups sugar
    2 T lemon juice

Measure fruit in large sauce pan. Add 2 cups sugar, boil hard for five minutes, stirring all the time. Add lemon juice and rest of sugar. Boil hard till thick as desired. Fast boiling holds the color of fruit. Skim off foam. Cool briefly, pack in jars. Pour hot paraffin on after cleaning neck of jar. Seal with hot lids.

PEACH JELLY

2 cups peach juice   1 T lemon juice
1 T fruit pectin   2 3/4 cups sugar

Heat peach juice and lemon juice with fruit pectin. Add sugar. Boil to a rolling boil for 1 minute. Skim off foam. Strain through piece of nylon hose into jelly glasses. Cool, then add melted paraffin to seal.

MINT JELLY

Get fresh mint leaves, simmer in enough water to cover leaves. Strain 1/3 cup mint water. Add enough water to make 1 1/3 cups in all. Add 2 1/2 T fruit pectin, bring to a boil. Add juice of a large lemon. Add 2 cups sugar. Put in large pan and boil one minute. Add a few drops green food coloring. Skim off foam. Strain through nylon into jelly glasses. Cool, cover with melted paraffin to seal.

PEACH BUTTER

Peel and seed 2 lb. good ripe peaches. Grind in food chopper. Measure into large sauce pan, then add equal parts of sugar. Add half of sugar and cook to boil, stirring all the time. Then add last of sugar and 2 T lemon juice. Boil quickly till it is thick but not jelled. Can while hot.

I used this recipe in 1973 and 1974, and won first both years and also won a trophy both years.

PLUM BUTTER

Use red ripe plums. Wash and cook whole, add just enough water to keep from sticking. When very soft run through colander removing seeds. Measure into sauce pan and add equal parts of sugar, stir and cook quickly. Boil about 10 - 15 minutes, but not to jell stage. Seal in jars while hot.

Use good flavored red plums. With this recipe, I win each year.

APRICOT MARMALADE

Peel and chop 1 1/2 lbs. apricots. In a large pan make a syrup of 1 1/2 lbs. sugar and 1 cup water. Drop fruit in boiling syrup. Put asbestos pad under pan to keep from sticking. Boil and stir, skim off foam. Boil till thick, about 10 - 15 minutes. Cool briefly and can in sterilized jars using sterilized lids.

A good winner.

•|•

PICKLES and RELISHES

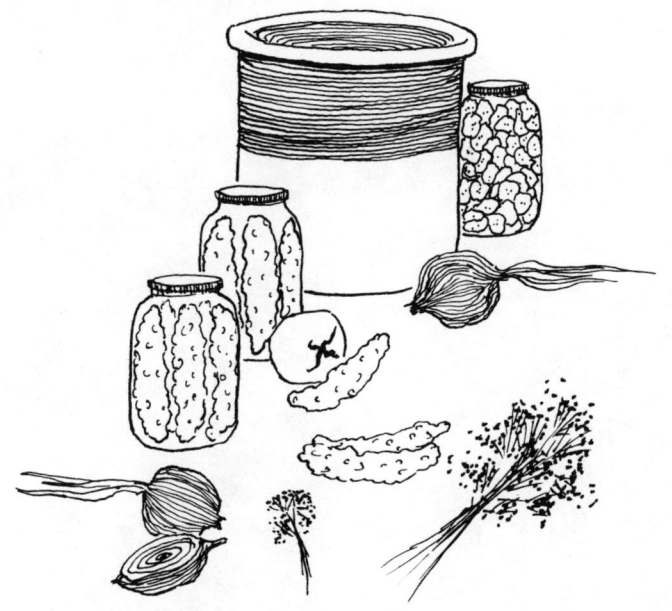

PICKLES AND RELISHES

SWEET CUCUMBER PICKLES

Wash about 1 gallon small cucumbers. Put in stone jar or large granite bucket. To one gallon of boiling hot water, add 1 pint of salt and dissolve salt before pouring over cucumbers. Cover container, let stand 1 week, in cool place. Drain and cover with 1 gallon hot water with 1 T powdered ammonium alum. Let stand 24 hours. Drain and cover with boiling water, let stand 24 hours. Then drain. Puncture each cucumber with long needle or hat pin. Prepare the following:

2 1/2 quarts vinegar	6 cups sugar
1 T celery seed	1 stick cinnamon bark
1 T cloves	

Let all come to boil, add to cucumbers. Let stand 3 days. Drain off and save mixture. Add 1 cup sugar, heat mixture again and add to cucumbers. Then let stand 3 days more and repeat till 2 more cups of sugar are added. When the last of the sugar is added, can in glass jars.
Very good, an all time winner.

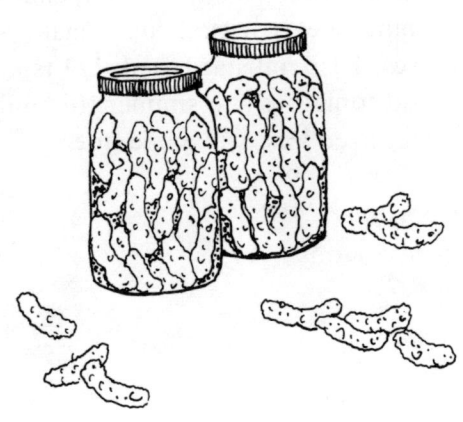

CRISP DILL PICKLES

Mix and bring these ingredients to a boil:
- 3 quarts water
- 1 quart white vinegar
- 1/4 tsp. powdered ammonium alum
- 1 cup salt
- 1/3 cup dill seed

Place washed cucumbers in sterilized jars. Use either whole or sliced cucumbers. Pour hot liquid over cucumbers in jars and seal with sterilized lids. If cucumbers are used whole, stick the long way with a long needle or hat pin. If any liquid is left over, save it in a jar and use when you have more cucumbers. Remember to reheat liquid before using.

A prize winner.

GREEN TOMATO PICKLES

Slice 1/2 gallon green tomatoes, add 1/4 cup salt to enough water to cover tomatoes. Let stand overnight. Drain, and rinse salt off tomatoes. Heat 2/3 pint vinegar with 2 cups sugar. Add 1 stick of cinnamon, 1 tsp. cloves, 1 tsp. mustard seed, 1/4 tsp. powdered ammonium alum. Add tomatoes and simmer till tender. Can in sterilized jars using sterilized lids, seal while hot.

Always a good prize winner.

BREAD AND BUTTER PICKLES

    1 doz. medium large cucumbers
    3 or 4 onions

Slice these both about 1/4 inch thick, let stand 1 hour in salt water, drain.

Mix:

2 cups vinegar	2 tsp. tumeric
2 1/2 cups sugar	2 tsp. mustard seed
1/2 tsp. pepper	2 tsp. celery seed

Heat all together, add cucumbers and onions and cook slowly, 45 - 60 minutes, don't boil. Seal while hot.

Won many times on this recipe as well as in 1974 and 1975.

❖❘❖

WATERMELON PICKLES

Prepare 3 lb. of rind by peeling and cutting chunks. Soak a few hours in weak salt water. Drain liquid. Cover with water in sauce pan. Cook till chunks are clear and tender. Add 5 cups sugar, 3/4 cup vinegar, 1 stick cinnamon bark, 1 tsp. whole cloves, 1 lemon sliced. Cook all slowly for about 30 minutes. Seal in sterilized jars.

1974 and 1975 first prize winner.

PEACH PICKLES

Select 4 pounds of medium yellow peaches (clingstones are best). Peel and leave whole.

Prepare a syrup of:

    2 lb. sugar   1/2 cup vinegar
    2 cups water   1 stick whole cinnamon
    1 tsp. whole cloves   bark

Heat syrup to boiling, add peaches, cook slowly stirring to turn over peaches. Cook till peaches look like they are cooked through and clear. Skim off foam. Can while hot and seal.

PEPPER HASH

  12 peppers — 4 red, 4 yellow, 4 green
    1 head cabbage
    6 onions

Grind peppers and cabbage. Soak overnight in salt water. Drain. In the morning grind onions, add to peppers and cabbage.

Mix:

    1 T mustard seed   1 T celery seed
  1 1/2 pints vinegar   1 1/4 pints sugar

Add peppers, cabbage, and onion mixture. Cook all till done, about 30 minutes. Can and seal while hot.

CARROT & CUCUMBER RELISH

6 large cucumbers	2 cups sugar
6 medium carrots	2 T salt
2 medium onions	1 1/2 T celery seed
1 cup vinegar	1 1/2 T mustard seed
1 cup water	

Grind all vegetables, sprinkle with salt, let stand 3 hours, drain. Bring vinegar, water and sugar to a boil then add vegetables and spices. Simmer 20 to 30 minutes. Seal while hot in sterilized jars. Makes 2-1/2 pints.

•I•

CELERY RELISH

1 pint celery, cut up	1 cup vinegar
1 pint chopped onion	1 cup water
2 green peppers, chopped	2/3 cup sugar
1 red pepper, chopped	1 T mustard seed

Cook all together over slow heat, till clear and tender, about 30 minutes. Have jars and lids sterilized and hot. Can while hot and seal.

Very good.

HOT DOG RELISH

2 1/2 cups ground cucumbers	1 1/2 cups ground onions
1 1/2 cups ground celery	1 green pepper, chopped
1 hot red pepper, chopped	1/3 cup salt
3 cups water	1 pint vinegar
1 1/2 cups sugar	1 tsp. white mustard seed
1 tsp. celery seed	

Cook all together till onions look done, about one hour. Cook slowly. Can while hot.

Try this one, good on hot dogs, also a Fair winner.

TWO POUND RELISH

2 lb. ripe tomatoes	2 lb. red ripe apples, unpeeled
2 lb. onions	
1 tsp. salt	2 lb. sugar (scant)
2 T mixed spice (in bag)	2 cups vinegar

Chop tomatoes, onions and apples. Put all ingredients together in large kettle. Cook slowly till clear, about 45 minutes. Can while hot in glass jars and seal.

Yes, I have won on this one.

CORN RELISH

1 pint of corn cut from cob	1 cup chopped cabbage
1/2 cup chopped red pepper	1/2 cup chopped onion
1/2 cup chopped green pepper	1/2 tsp. tumeric powder (or more)
1/2 tsp. celery seed	
1 tsp. dry mustard powder	1/2 cup water
3/4 cup vinegar	3/4 cup sugar

Put all ingredients in sauce pan, cook slowly about 30 - 45 minutes. Have pint jars and lids sterilized. Seal while hot.

Won in 1974 and 1975, also many times before.

HOME CANNING

HOME CANNING

CANNED CORN

Select nice, tender, fresh corn. Blanch on cob in hot water (just bring to boil). Cut corn from cob, fill jars to the neck of jar loosely. Add hot water just to cover corn. Leave 1 inch space. Add salt if desired. Process in pressure cooker for 1 hour and 15 minutes at 5 lb. pressure. Note: I cook it for a longer time at less pressure for better flavor.
It has to be good canned this way!

CANNED CARROTS

Select nice crisp carrots. Peel and leave whole the length of the jar. Blanch in boiling water for 15 minutes. Place in hot sterilized jars. Add salt and hot water to carrots, seal lids tight. Process by directions of pressure cooker. Cook 45 minutes at 5 lb. pressure.

Won in 1974 and 1975.

CANNED BEETS

Cook small tender beets in boiling water till peeling will slip off. Pack in sterilized hot jars and fill to neck of jar. Fill with boiling water 1/2 inch from top. Add 1 tsp. salt to each quart jar. Tighten lid, process in pressure cooker by pressure directions for 50 minutes at 5 lb. pressure.

This recipe won Blue Ribbons for several years at the State Fair and also won in 1975.

CANNED GREEN BEANS

Pick tender green beans and break in pieces or can whole. Wash and pack in hot sterilized jars. Fill with boiling water (I use rain water) to 1 inch from top of jar. Add 1 tsp. coarse salt per quart jar. Process in pressure cooker according to directions, for 1 hour at 5 lb. pressure. Remove cooker from heat, let cool till pressure goes to zero. Then open slowly and remove jars and place on rack to cool out of a draft.

I always can by this recipe for home use, also a big winner at Fairs.

CANNED PEAS

Select young tender peas. Blanch hulled peas in boiling water about 10 minutes. Fill sterilized jars to the neck of jar (don't crowd them for they swell some). Fill jar with boiling water to top of peas. Add salt if desired, 1 tsp. to a quart. Clean top of jar neck free of juices, salt etc. Have lids boiling hot. To cook in pressure cooker, follow instructions of cooker. Cook 1 hour at 5 lb. pressure.

Yes, I won on this recipe in 1974 and 1975.

•I•

CANNED TOMATOES

Peel whole tomatoes, or cut large ones in chunks. Use sterilized jars and lids. Pack cold tomatoes in jars and fill to 1 inch from top with boiling water. Add 1 tsp. salt to each quart. Seal tight and place in heavy aluminum container or stone jar on rack in bottom. Fill container with boiling water to the top of the lids. Put lid on top of container and wrap container with a rug or blanket. Leave all day or overnight. If you have a good seal, they will keep indefinitely.

This recipe is always a winner.

CANNED CHERRIES

Seed nice, ripe cherries, leave them whole. Make syrup of 3/4 cup water and 1/2 cup sugar, heat and put in enough cherries for 1 pint jar. Simmer to heat fruit. Place in jar and fill with juice to 1/2 inch from top of jar. Put in pressure cooker with about 2 lb. pressure for 5 minutes to get a good seal.

Ever try seeding with an old fashioned hair pin?

Select nice red, ripe cherries. I have won first with this recipe so many times.

•|•

CANNED RASPBERRIES OR BLACKBERRIES

Select firm, ripe berries, place in sterilized jars. Make syrup of one part of sugar to two parts of water. Fill jar with syrup, all but full, and place lid on tight. Put in pressure cooker, process at 2 lb. pressure for 5 minutes. Test when cold to be sure of a perfect seal.

HOUSEHOLD HINTS and HOMEMADE SOAP

HOUSEHOLD HINTS AND HOMEMADE SOAPS

Beat an egg and brush over breads, rolls and nut breads just before taking from oven.

Use rain water for canning fruits and vegetables to make them crystal clear and sparkle.

When measuring shortening, if recipe calls for 1/2 cup, first fill measuring cup 1/2 full of water then fill full of shortening.

When creaming shortening and sugar, if recipe calls for soda, add it and cream all together.

When cooking Seven Minute Icing, add 1 tsp. of plain gelatin dissolved in 1 T of water. Beat in when finished cooking.

Have trouble creaming shortening and sugar with mixer? I always warm the bowl and sugar in oven, with the pilot on. The shortening should be soft, but not melted.

To have clear liquids when canning fruits and vegetables, strain juice through pieces of nylon hose.

When beating egg yolks, add a little milk or water to beat.

Strain hot jelly into containers through nylon hose squares.

I always sift flour before measuring to be accurate.

Cook a slice of lemon with sweet potatoes to keep them from turning dark.

Make sour milk by adding 1 T lemon juice or vinegar to sweet milk.

1 tsp. vinegar added to home made noodles, makes them tender.

Warm knife over low burner to cut cheese.

Use powdered sugar to sweeten whipped cream to keep it from becoming watery.

Use Teflon coated cookie pans to make baking easier.

When baking butter cakes, I always grease bottom of pans, then dust them with flour, and put waxed paper over that.

HOME MADE SOAP I

4 level tablespoons lye
1 cup rain water
2 cups melted and strained fat (use lard or bacon grease, strained)
2 tablespoons powdered borax

Dissolve lye in water in a stone container or heavy granite pan. Put melted fat in granite pan or stone container and pour lye solution very slowly into fat, stirring all the time with wooden paddle. Stir in the borax and keep stirring unit it thickens. Pour in teacups or glass dishes, leave till it hardens.

◆I◆

HOME MADE SOAP II

6 lb. grease   1 can lye
3 quarts rain water   2 tablespoons powdered borax

Use melted and strained bacon grease drippings. Use a large granite dish pan or stone jar. Put grease in first, then pour dry lye over grease and mix well. Add rain water slowly, a quart at a time and stir. Stir well but slowly. Add borax and mix well. Stir every once-in-a-while until it sets. Leave it alone till firm enough to cut in cakes.

Yes, I have even made home made soap and won first prizes.

Index

CAKES, 33-52
  Angel Food Cake, 41
  Applesauce Cake I, 39
  Applesauce Cake II, 40
  Burnt Sugar Cake, 36
  Cake of the Golden West, 47
  Carrot Pineapple Cake, 50
    Frosting, 50
  Chocolate Angel Food Cake, 40
  Chocolate Marshmallow Roll, 43
    Icing, 43
  Coconut White Cake, 35
  Creamy Pineapple Icing, 44
  Dark Fruit Cake, 52
    Glaze, 52
  Devil's Food Cake, 37
  Hickory Nut Cake, 36
  Jelly Roll, 37
  Kentucky Cream Cake, 39
    Frosting, 39
  Lazy Daisy Cake, 47
    Topping, 47
  Lemon Filling, 38
  Lemon Yellow Cake, 38
    Filling, 38
  My Mother's Soft
    Gingerbread, 42
  Never Fail Cupcakes, 48
  Orange Candy Surprise Cake, 45
    Glazes, 45
  Peanut Butter Cake, 51
    Topping, 51
  Pineapple Cake, 46
    Filling, 46
  Pineapple Chiffon Cake, 44
    Icing, 44
  Pineapple Coconut Cupcakes, 49
    Frosting, 49
  Pineapple Upside Down Cake, 42
  Prune Cake, 41
  Rainbow Cakettes, 48

CANDIES, 83-86
  Aunt Bill's Brown Candy, 86
  Chocolate Fudge, 85
  Divinity Candy, 86
  Peanut Brittle, 85
  Popcorn Crisps, 86

CASSEROLES AND SOUP, 87-94
  Chicken Divan, 91
  Chicken Vegetable Casserole, 89
  Macaroni and Cheese, 92
  Noodles, 94
  Onions Baked in
    Tomato Juice, 93
  Salmon Egg Casserole, 93
  Salmon Patties, 91
  Scalloped Chicken, 92
  Scalloped Corn, 89
  Sweet Potato Casserole, 90
  Turkey Loaf, 90
  Vegetable Soup, 94

COOKIES AND BARS, 19-32
   Apple Walnut Squares, 32
      Icing, 32
   Boiled Raisin Cookies, 23
   Chocloate Ice Box Cookies, 24
   Chocolate Krinkle Cookies, 28
   Chocolate Raisin Cookies, 27
   Cloud Nine Butterscotch Bars, 31
      Frosting, 31
   Coconut Macaroons, 26
   Date Nut Bars, 31
   Filled Cookies, 29
      Filling, 29
   German Fruit Cookies, 21
   Ginger Cookies, (Frosted), 22
   Ice Box Cookies, 24
   Kisses, 27
   Mother's Best Oatmeal Cookies, 25
   Mother's Sugar Cookies, 29
   Oat Krispies, 28
   Oatmeal Date Cookies, 26
   Peanut Butter Cookies, 22
   Pinwheel Cookies, 30
      Filling, 30
   Sour Milk Doughnuts, 32
   Sugar Drops, 25
   Tiger Cookies, 23

DESERTS AND SALADS, 77-82
   Cream Puffs, 82
   Dessert Cherry Salad, 79
   Golden Apricot Salad, 80
   Graham Cracker Cheese Cake, 81
   Jello Salad, 80
   Marshmallow Salad, 79
   Pudding Jello, 81

HOME CANNING, 111-116
   Canned Beets, 114
   Canned Carrots, 113
   Canned Cherries, 116
   Canned Corn, 113
   Canned Green Beans, 114
   Canned Peas, 115
   Canned Raspberries or Blackberries, 116
   Canned Tomatoes, 115

HONEY RECIPES, 67-76
   Carrot Honey Cookeis, 73
   Honey Nut Bread, 72
   Honey Devil's Food Cake, 70
      Icing, 70
   Honey Fruit Bars, 71
   Honey Ginger Bread, 72
   Honey Hermits, 73
   Honey Icing, 70
   Honey Oatmeal Cookies, 74
   Honey Raisin Bread, 76
   Honey Rye Bread, 75
   Honey Spice Cake, 69
      Icing, 69
   Honey White Bread, 75
   Honey Whole Wheat Bread, 76
   Spicy Pineapple Honey Glaze for Ham, 74
   White Honey Cake, 71

HOUSEHOLD HINTS AND HOMEMADE SOAP, 117-120
   Hints, 119-120
   Homemade Soap I and II, 120

ICINGS, 53-56
   Butter Cream Frosting, 56
   Butter Icing, 55
   Caramel Icing, 56
   Chocolate Icing, 55
   Orange Glaze, 56
   Seven Minute Icing, 55

PICKLES AND RELISHES, 103-110
   Bread and Butter Pickles, 107
   Carrot & Cucumber Relish, 109
   Celery Relish, 109
   Corn Relish, 110
   Crisp Dill Pickles, 106
   Green Tomato Pickles, 106
   Hot Dog Relish, 110

Peach Pickles, 108
Pepper Hash, 108
Sweet Cucumber Pickles, 105
Two Pound Relish, 110
Watermelon Pickles, 107

PIES AND COBBLERS, 57-66
 Apple Cobbler, 61
 Apple Pie With Coconut
   Crumb Top, 60
   Crumb Topping, 60
 Chiffon Pumpkin Pie, 64
 Chocolate Chip Pie, 63
 Lemon Pie, 60
 Meringue for Cream Pies, 66
 Mincemeat, 64
 Never Fail Pie Crust, 66
 Peach Cobbler, 59
 Peach Crumble, 65
   Topping, 65
 Pumpkin Pie, 63
 Raisin Cream Pie, 61
 Rhubarb Pie With Meringue, 62

PRESERVES, JAMS, JELLIES
 AND BUTTERS, 95-102
 Apricot Marmalade, 102
 Apricot Preserves, 97
 Basic Jam Recipe, 99
 Cherry Preserves, 98
 Mint Jelly, 100
 Peach Butter, 101
 Peach Jelly, 100
 Peach Preserves, 97

Plum Butter, 101
Strawberry Jam, 99
Strawberry Preserves, 98

QUICK BREADS, 11-18
 Best Ever Banana Bread, 13
 Bran Muffins, 14
 Cheese Sticks, 18
 Corn Muffins, 15
 Graham Muffins, 15
 Nut Bread, 14
 Quick Coffee Cake, 16
   Topping, 16
 Raised Doughnuts, 17
   Glaze, 17
 Steamed Boston Brown Bread, 13

YEAST BREADS, 1-10
 Cheese Bread, 4
 Cinnamon Rolls, 8
 Cinnamon Swirl Orange
   Bread, 4
 Coffee Cake, 9
   Topping, 9
 Compressed Yeast Bread, 5
 Danish Pastry, 7
 Dinner Rolls, 7
 English Tea Muffins, 10
 Frosted Currant Bread, 3
   Icing, 3
 Parker House Rolls, 6
 Potato White Bread, 5
 Refrigerator Rolls, 8
 Rye Bread, 10
 Whole Wheat Bread, 6

NOTES